Pollution Prevention Opportunity Assessments

A Handbook for Business

Jill A. Engel-Cox and Kim M. Fowler

Blue Agama
Books

Disclaimer

Because it is not possible to envision the conditions under which this information will be used, neither the authors, nor Battelle, makes any warranty or representation expressed or implied, that use of the methods discussed herein will be successful in complying with local, state, federal, or international laws and regulations, or that such would be safe. Those using this information must assure themselves that they are operating safely and within the law. This document is intended to serve as a resource, but not as a substitute for legal advice or good judgment.

An earlier version of this book was published in 1999 by Battelle Press as "Pollution Prevention Opportunity Assessments for Research & Development Laboratories." This version has been significantly modified to make it broadly applicable to businesses of all kinds.

ePub ISBN 978-0-9905179-0-0
MOBI ISBN 978-0-9905179-1-7
Print On Demand ISBN 978-0-9905179-8-6

Blue Agama Books
Golden, Colorado
+1 657-333-2112
www.blueagama.com/books

CONTENTS

Acknowledgements

We, the authors, would like to thank the people who helped make this book possible. We especially want to thank the students of Johns Hopkins University Industrial Pollution Prevention and Cleaner Production classes, who provided inspiration through the assessments they completed with small businesses. Special thanks to Ms. Sabina Pennington, who graciously allowed her work to be used as the basis for the general example in this document, and to the veterinary clinic she worked with. We would especially like to acknowledge and thank Ms. Christina M. Mausser of Pittny Creative for her excellent work preparing the cover and the example icon and Mr. Michael Perkins for the process graphic. Finally, we want to thank Mr. Glen Engel-Cox for his valuable time to review the document and to help us through the electronic publishing process. Ultimately, any remaining errors or idiosyncrasies remain ours, but their help in improving our text as a whole is appreciated.

Introduction
Chapter 1

Get Started

Collect Information

Brainstorm

Analyze

Make Recommendation

Implement

Document

1. *Choose a diverse team, including a champion to lead the assessment.*
2. *Gather data about key waste generating activities by identifying the material, energy and water use, quantifying waste streams, and walking through the facility spaces where activities are being conducted.*
3. *Brainstorm pollution prevention opportunities.*
4. *Research and analyze pollution prevention opportunities for waste reduction, energy savings, cost savings, and return on investment.*
5. *Make recommendations for pollution prevention implementation projects based on the waste, energy, and cost analysis.*
6. *Document your work and implement the opportunities.*

Reducing waste, material use, energy use, water use, and cost in an organization can be achieved more effectively when operations are reviewed methodically and when a business' employees are engaged. Pollution prevention opportunity assessments are a method that offers structure and an engagement strategy that has been successful in identifying resource optimization strategies for many different types of organizations.

The authors have used the *pollution prevention opportunity assessments* at their workplaces and at businesses of all sizes, and as a teaching tool to identify ways to reduce pollution and avoid costs. The U.S. Environmental Protection Agency originally developed a pollution prevention opportunity assessment method for manufacturers, calling them "waste minimization opportunity assessments." The U.S. Department of Energy later called their first version of the U.S. Environmental Protection Agency method "process waste assessments." We have modified the assessment approach to address multiple settings ranging from small businesses to schools to health care operations. The assessment process is a simple, systematic method to identify pollution prevention opportunities, evaluate the impact they could have on operations, and document the results to assist with implementation. The techniques and assessments detailed in this handbook were initially implemented at the Pacific Northwest National Laboratory and subsequently used by students at several universities to identify resource optimization strategies for small and medium-sized businesses and schools.

This introductory chapter covers basic concepts, such as describing pollution prevention, discussing what a pollution prevention opportunity assessment is, noting the benefits of assessments, and showing how they fit into a pollution prevention program. Each subsequent chapter covers a step in the pollution prevention opportunity assessment process. At the beginning of each chapter is a list of the activities to complete that step. Each chapter also includes an example from a completed pollution prevention opportunity assessment. The full example assessment report is included in the appendix.

What is Pollution Prevention?

The first approach to preventing pollution is *source reduction*—reducing energy, water, and materials use at the source before it becomes waste. This is the easiest and most cost-effective way to eliminate or at least reduce waste in your operations, since no waste would have to be treated, boxed or barreled if it is not generated in the first place. Source reduction may mean replacing a waste producing process with another cleaner process, such as substituting small individualized containers with bulk materials to eliminate packaging waste. It may mean finding ways to do work electronically instead of with chemicals,

Pollution Prevention Techniques

The hierarchy of source reduction, reuse/recycle, treatment, and disposal is an easy way to categorize some of the common pollution prevention techniques used in businesses.

Source Reduction

- **Go electronic**: Replace a process that historically was performed with chemicals with one that can be performed on a computer.
- **Substitute materials**: Replace a hazardous substance with a non-hazardous substance. Look for environmentally preferable materials made from rapidly renewable or biobased products.
- **Modernize equipment**: Review the equipment catalogs to see if the up-to-date versions of your equipment use less energy, water, materials and/or generate less waste.
- **Reduce the scale**: Reduce the quantity of resources used and or perform the activity at a smaller scale using new techniques or technology.
- **Redesign the process**: Modify the procedures of a process to reduce the number of steps and to incorporate other source reduction opportunities.
- **Manage inventories**: Order only those chemicals needed to perform the work in the quantity needed now; that is, do not order in bulk just because the chemical purchasing cost appears to be less expensive.
- **Segregate materials**: Keep hazardous and non-hazardous materials separate to avoid contamination.
- **Practice good housekeeping**: Keep the work space clean, redistribute or dispose of materials when they are no longer needed, maintain equipment so that they are working at their optimal performance level.

Reuse/Recycling

- **Close the Loop**: Modify the process so that the waste outputs can be used as inputs.
- **Exchange materials**: Communicate with other staff about the availability and/or need for specific chemicals and materials so that excess materials can be used by others instead of being disposed of as waste.
- **Use reusable equipment**: Use materials that can be cleaned and reused versus disposable materials.
- **Recycle the recyclables**: Where materials cannot be reused, coordinate with local recyclers or vendors for a recycling program that accepts the materials you are using.
- **Purchase supplies that are recyclable and that contain recycled content**: Items that contain recycled content should be purchased where possible so that a continued market for recycling exists. If one-time use is required, purchase items that can be recycled and/or items made from environmentally preferable materials.

Treatment

- **Neutralize:** Adjust the pH of a liquid waste stream so that it is no longer considered hazardous and can be disposed into the sewer. Regulatory approval is required for onsite treatment of hazardous waste.
- **Evaporate:** Remove the water from the waste stream prior to disposal. This technique reduces volume but often increases the toxicity of the now concentrated waste. Regulatory approval is required for onsite treatment of hazardous waste.
- **Compact:** Reduce the volume of the wastes by crushing it into a smaller volume prior to disposal.
- **Recover waste:** Turn end-of-the-pipe waste into a sellable product.

Disposal

- **Document**: Carefully record all of the constituents of the materials you will dispose of to ensure proper characterization and disposal.
- **Coordinate with waste management staff:** Submit your waste and all documentation to waste management personnel and ask them any questions you may have about storage, documentation, or handling.

such as using digital cameras instead of film-developing processes. Or reducing electricity demand by using more efficient equipment.

The second approach is *reuse and recycling*—reusing chemicals and materials or reprocessing instead of disposing of them. Reusing or redistributing chemicals and materials can save thousands of dollars in purchase and disposal costs, as well as facilitate good chemical management. Recycling can be done onsite, such as with solvent distillation units for more consistent chemical waste streams, or through contracts with outside vendors, such as for oil re-refining or battery regeneration. Often, these recycling techniques and contracts can be done without additional costs since the material being recycled has value. Purchasing environmentally preferable products closes the loop. Purchasing materials made from recycled content increases the market for these products and makes the recycled materials more valuable to the vendor.

When source reduction, reusing, and recycling are not feasible, *treatment* is an option—reducing the toxicity or volume of waste before safely disposing of it. Neutralizing chemicals is one direct way of accomplishing this. Considerable savings in disposal fees have been possible after hazardous waste is made suitable for process sewer disposal. Often, treatment can be done onsite with common equipment and processes, once regulatory approval has been received.

What is a Pollution Prevention Opportunity Assessment?

A *pollution prevention opportunity assessment* is a systematic, documented approach to determine where pollution prevention opportunities exist. Once opportunities are identified, the assessment can also reveal the best means of implementing the opportunity. The assessment maps out future pollution prevention activities and savings opportunities so that continuous improvement of operations is the focus.

A pollution prevention opportunity assessment also helps determine the cost of the present energy, water, and materials use, the cost of waste management and disposal, the cost of changing to a cleaner process, the cost savings of a cleaner or more efficient system, and the time needed to repay your investment. Determining the cost impacts of waste streams is an essential part of the pollution prevention process. The assessment can point toward innovative or emerging technologies that will be cleaner, safer, and more cost-effective, and will sometimes improve operations.

The steps to completing an assessment are basic but effective (see Figure 1). They are detailed in the chapters of this handbook:

1. Choose a diverse team, including a champion to lead the assessment.
2. Gather data about key waste generating activities by identifying the material, energy and water use, quantifying waste streams, and walking through the facility spaces where activities are being conducted.
3. Brainstorm pollution prevention opportunities.
4. Research and analyze pollution prevention opportunities for waste reduction, energy savings, cost savings, and return on investment.
5. Make recommendations for pollution prevention implementation projects based on the waste, energy, and cost analysis.
6. Document your work and implement the opportunities.

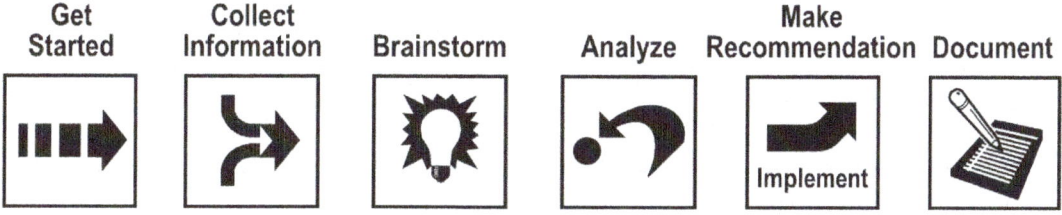

Figure 1. Steps in a Pollution Prevention Assessment.

Why Do a Pollution Prevention Opportunity Assessment?

The benefits of including pollution prevention in business operations have been well documented. A pollution prevention opportunity assessment results in recommendations to reduce material, energy, and water use, and reduce waste that result in the following:

- *Cost savings,* including reduced material purchase costs, reduced chemical management and waste disposal costs, reduced regulatory requirements and compliance costs, and increased data quality and work efficiency.
- *Safety improvements and risk reduction,* including reduced staff exposure to chemicals and reduced potential for accidents and spills
- *Process efficiency,* including more efficient use of raw materials and energy, and better design of business processes
- *Environmental stewardship,* including reduced potential for releases to the environment, reduced material, water, and energy consumption, reduced waste generation, and reduced ecological degradation

- *Good public relations,* including reduced inventories and releases reported, increased positive activities to share with community, and improved relations with regulators
- *Enhanced business operations,* including improved quality and quantity of output by utilizing new technologies or processes.

How Do Assessments Fit into a Bigger Picture?

Pollution prevention opportunity assessments are powerful tools for learning more about operational activities and determining ways to reduce waste and save money. The intent of performing an assessment is to identify which pollution prevention opportunities should be implemented and which are not beneficial or cost-effective. Without implementation, a pollution prevention opportunity assessment is merely another paper study and no waste will be reduced. Pollution prevention opportunity assessments are most effective with management engagement and the support of key stakeholders.

Pollution prevention opportunity assessments can be part of a comprehensive pollution prevention program. A program can include financial and institutional incentives that encourage staff to initiate pollution prevention activities, including management support and a cost chargeback system. It also provides the technical support to help staff find the resources and information to implement the opportunities recommended by their assessments and recognizes them for their positive work. In turn, pollution prevention opportunity assessments are critical to achieving larger goals for a pollution prevention program, especially helping foster a culture change among staff, allowing them to think about their work in terms of its impact on the environment.

An Overall Pollution Prevention Philosophy

The key to conducting assessments and reducing waste is to remember that offices, businesses, and classrooms are filled with intelligent and creative people who care about their work and its potential impact on the environment and their community. When given dedicated work time, technical assistance, a basic assessment methodology, and the freedom to review their own activities, staff will develop creative solutions to reduce the waste they generate and the materials, water, and energy they use.

How to Use This Handbook

Chapters 2 through 7 contain step-by-step instructions on how to perform a pollution prevention opportunity assessment. The instructions include a short list of tasks, a descriptive discussion on how to perform the tasks, and an illustrative example for each of the steps. Chapter 8 summarizes the whole process and the appendix provides the complete final pollution prevention opportunity assessment report for the example used throughout chapters 2 through 7. The handbook should be used as a guide to conducting an assessment, yet should be considered flexible enough to meet your organization's needs and resource constraints.

Background Information for the Example

Veterinary clinics and animal hospitals are very common small businesses which produce a variety of hazardous, non-hazardous, and medical waste. The Animal Hospital in this example is a composite based on assessments conducted as part of a class on pollution prevention. The students, as pollution prevention specialists, worked with actual small businesses to conduct pollution prevention assessments.

The Animal Hospital is a community veterinary clinic that provides routine and emergency care for small domestic animals. Services include vaccinations, onsite routine blood laboratory testing, x-rays, chemotherapy, geriatric care, emergency care, surgeries such as spay/neuter, infection/abscess treatments, dental cleaning, and doctor house calls. The facility has a staff of 8 professional personnel consisting of one veterinary physician, one office manager, one receptionist and 5 support/ veterinary assistants. This facility sees approximately 140 patients per week, with surgeries/dental cleanings conducted about 3 days per week. When meeting with the pollution prevention specialist, the owner of the Animal Hospital was particularly concerned with the x-ray machine, which produced chemical waste. Although disposed of correctly through a vendor, it was a waste stream of particular concern.

The owner and staff were interested in the following goals for the assessment:

- Reduce waste of all kinds
- Save energy
- Reduce cost
- Improve working conditions
- Appeal to customers through green operations

The process and results of this assessment are presented at end of each chapter as an example. The experiences of the Animal Hospital are used to describe each of the pollution prevention opportunity assessment steps.

Get Started
Chapter 2

Get Started   Collect Information   Brainstorm   Analyze   Make Recommendation   Document

1. *Establish the scope of the assessment.*
2. *Secure financial resources.*
3. *Gain management support.*
4. *Identify the team leader and the assessment team.*
5. *Assign a pollution prevention specialist.*
6. *Set a schedule and kick-off the assessment.*

In the early stages of assessments, team members often encounter resistance from their peers: "We don't generate that much waste" or "We are already doing everything we can." Typically, they may have made some changes to their business processes, picking the opportunities that are easy to implement— the low-hanging fruit. However, by the time the assessments have ended, these same staff are approaching management in order to implement new pollution prevention activities. The assessment process can uncover a range of new possibilities that reduce energy use, prevent waste, save money, and improve operations or product delivery. New technologies and processes are always being developed, therefore finding alternatives that both reduce waste and enhance operations requires a commitment to continuous improvement.

The early steps of establishing a scope, securing funding, getting management support, forming a team, and setting up the assessment are essential to the likelihood of successful waste reduction.

Establish the Scope of the Assessment

The scope or the boundaries of the assessment should be structured to fit the needs of the business and those performing the assessment. The scope is those activities and/or locations that the assessment will review. The scope can cover a single waste stream, a single business activity or process, a set of waste streams or processes, all the activities within an organization, or any combination of these. How the scope is set can depend on the nature of the waste streams, nature of business activities, physical location of work, number of staff involved, or all of the above.

Examples of pollution prevention opportunity assessment scope include:

- A department, technical group, or set of operations located in the same building
- A group of similar waste streams, business processes, or projects
- Waste streams, energy or water use from similar equipment used on various projects
- One-time, high levels of resource consumption, high waste volume projects that are occurring currently or in the near future (for example, inventory clean-outs, moves, new construction).

Ideally, the scope is not so large that more than 10 pollution prevention opportunities result from the assessment, or else the assessment may become too big and lose focus. Exceptions to this would be when most of the opportunities identified are easy. If the assessment scope seems too big for one team to handle in a reasonable time, the assessment can be split into two or more and conducted separately with different teams or over time.

Secure Financial Resources

Staff need time and expertise to conduct the assessments. Thus, they need to have resources for this time or expertise. The amount of time needed depends on the assessment scope and level of detail. For smaller businesses, one resource for performing the assessment could be college students enrolled in a pollution prevention, environmental science, or chemistry class, or working as part of a community-based program. Assessments completed as part of a course or program give students excellent hands-on experience and can be a low-cost way to complete the time-consuming information gathering and analysis portions of an assessment. When students conduct the assessment, however, care must be taken that an internal commitment is made by management to implement the results of the assessment. Grants or technical assistance for assessments may also be available through local or city regulatory agencies.

Gain Management Support

Without some level of management support, an assessment will not be as effective. Management support can come in several ways and at various levels. The most basic sort of support may be an agreement to conduct an assessment. Other forms of management support may include the manager being a part of the team, providing resources to do the assessment, providing resources to implement opportunities, and/or making completion of the assessment or

---

Critical Elements and Expectations to Start a Successful Assessment

Two elements are essential for a successful pollution prevention opportunity assessment:

- The assessment team is led by or includes a staff member who works in the area being assessed
- The assessment team is provided with the people and financial resources, a general methodology, and as much pollution prevention technical assistance as needed.

The leader and the team have two critical expectations to meet:

- Pollution prevention is the focus of the assessment, i.e., the team looks for opportunities to reduce at the source first, then, reuse/recycle, and finally treatment.
- The final product is the completed worksheets (discussed in Chapter 7).

implementation of pollution prevention a part of their performance goals. These levels of support feed each other as a business or department increases its depth of knowledge and enthusiasm for pollution prevention. Support may also increase with a group's ability to find resources to implement pollution prevention opportunities.

Identify the Team Leader and the Assessment Team

The team is the key to a successful pollution prevention opportunity assessment and implementation of pollution prevention projects. The selection of the team leader is very important and should be done first. The leader is often the instigator of the assessment, is a staff member or champion who is interested enough to volunteer, or is a good leader who has been chosen by management. Most importantly, the team leader needs to be a respected member of the parts of the organization that are being assessed. A respected team leader will provide the incentive and enthusiasm for implementation of the results of the assessment. The team leader identifies key wastes or processes to evaluate, rallies staff to provide data for the assessment, and recommends pollution prevention activities to management. It is up to the team leader to make sure that data are gathered and the pollution prevention opportunities are adequately investigated. The team leader needs to be a good organizer, willing to talk to management if issues arise, and to request implementation funding. The team leader needs to work with a diverse set of staff, such as compliance, waste management, and energy management staff.

Once the team leader is selected, they are responsible for forming the team. A team can be a formally structured or a loosely associated group of people who participate in portions of the assessment but not all of it. The team can include:

- *One to five key staff in the organization being assessed* - Staff participation is essential to this process. Staff are more likely to accept ideas and new ways of working when their colleagues have been involved in identifying pollution prevention opportunities. Teams should also include any staff who might significantly have to modify their work practices as a result of this assessment.
- *A pollution prevention specialist* – A pollution prevention specialist can provide a usable methodology, share pollution prevention technical information gained from past assessments, and facilitate meetings and brainstorming. The pollution prevention specialist can often offer technical expertise in uncovering pollution prevention opportunities that may no longer be visible to those who work in the space every day.

- *A management representative* - Managers can provide insight into the intent of practices or policies. Participating in the assessment, even if they only participate in the walkthrough and the brainstorming sessions, helps managers understand and support the team's recommendations and requests for implementation funds. Also, engaging managers in the day-to-day operations often gives them insight into the working conditions of staff and what it takes to get work done.

- *A waste management specialist* - Waste management specialists contribute knowledge of waste streams, including what happens to the waste once the operation is completed. This person can also provide assistance in researching the pollution prevention ideas.

- *An energy management specialist* – Energy management specialists contribute knowledge of energy efficient alternatives and strategies for energy conservation. This person also understands the cost implications of energy use changes.

- *An environmental compliance specialist* - To keep the team from introducing new ideas that raise compliance issues, an environmental compliance specialist can assist with background and research.

The assessment team should also invite participation from those interested in pollution prevention that could contribute to the scope of the assessment. Four to eight team members seem to work well, but larger teams with more members have also been successful. Team dynamics are worth considering for both effective implementation and the desired speed of the assessment.

Assign a Pollution Prevention Specialist

The pollution prevention specialist who is assigned to the pollution prevention opportunity assessment can provide the level of assistance that the team leader decides is appropriate. The specialist will help keep the focus of the assessment on pollution prevention and help ensure that the pollution prevention opportunity assessment worksheets are completed when the assessment is done (see Chapter 7). This can be a good role for a student.

Often, the pollution prevention specialist offers a wide range of assistance that includes:

- Identifying and refining the general scope of the assessment as defined by the team leader.
- Encouraging management involvement.
- Setting the assessment schedule with the team leader.

- Providing background information to assist with the assessment, such as previously performed assessments or waste generation data.
- Participating in the facility space walkthrough.
- Facilitating the brainstorming session.
- Researching pollution prevention opportunities at the request of the team leader.
- Reviewing and assisting with the completion of the worksheets.

The pollution prevention specialist can also be responsible for many of the administrative tasks, such as making sure the appropriate managers are aware the assessment is being performed, making the final assessment available for future reference, and helping prepare and submit implementation proposals where appropriate. The pollution prevention specialist may also follow up with the team to discover what was or was not implemented and what the measured costs and savings were once implemented.

However, do not generally expect the pollution prevention specialist to perform the entire assessment, collect all the data, or to be the team leader. The assessment needs to be the product of the team, so that they will implement the pollution prevention opportunities.

Set a Schedule and Kick-Off the Assessment

Once the pollution prevention opportunity assessment team has been named and the scope has been established, it is time to set the schedule and hold an assessment kick-off meeting. Scheduling may be affected by a variety of factors, but always involves working around the ongoing mission of the organization. Nevertheless, a schedule should follow a simple plan that is clear to team members and affected staff. For instance, a week-by-week schedule could look like this:

Week 0.	Management approves and assessment begins. Management assigns a team leader or a champion volunteers to lead the assessment.
Week 1.	Pollution prevention specialist provides a copy of this book, samples of previously performed assessments, and blank worksheets to the team leader. Team leader determines the team members and provides introductory materials to team members.
Week 2.	Team leader holds kick-off meeting attended by all team members. Initial data is collected.
Week 3.	Team completes draft version of Worksheets 1 and 2 (see Chapter 7). Team leader distributes completed draft copies of Worksheets 1 and 2 to team.

Week 4.	Team performs the walkthrough of facility spaces (1 to 2 hours). Pollution prevention specialist facilitates the brainstorming session (scheduled for at least 2 hours). Team leader assigns the research and completion of Worksheet 3 to team members.
Week 4-6.	Team researches and analyzes opportunities. Team completes drafts of Worksheet 3.
Week 6.	Team turns in drafts of Worksheet 3 to the team leader. Team leader distributes drafts of Worksheet 3 for comments.
Week 7.	Team leader prepares drafts of Worksheets 4 and 5.
Week 8.	Team leader incorporates Worksheet 3 comments into the draft document. Team leader distributes a complete draft of the completed pollution prevention opportunity assessment to the entire team.
Week 9.	Team leader incorporates final comments.
Week 10.	Team completes assessment and presents results to management and others.

The kick-off meeting is held with the entire team and is intended to make sure everyone understands the process. During the meeting, the pollution prevention specialist provides an overview of the process. The team leader describes the general scope and schedule for the assessment. The leader also asks for suggestions to refine the assessment scope and solicits information on key waste streams, processes, facility spaces, and projects on which the team thinks they should focus their efforts.

When the schedule is set and the kick-off meeting has taken place, now the assessment can begin.

Example

Since the Animal Hospital was relatively small, all of their operations were included in the assessment. The owner was supportive of the assessment since he wanted to reduce waste and energy use, as well as reduce the cost of his operations. All the assessment team members were volunteers so there was no direct cost to conducting the assessment itself. A pollution prevention specialist led the assessment as part of an engineering class on pollution prevention and clean industry. She was knowledgeable about the pollution prevention process, chemicals and waste, and energy management. The owner of the Animal Hospital, who was also the senior veterinarian, and the office manager served as key members of the team. Other input was received from outside pollution prevention experts, as well as the rest of the staff at the Animal Hospital.

The pollution prevention specialist first met with the owner to explain the process and to hear his concerns and areas of interest. Then they developed the following schedule:

March 3.	Complete planning to conduct assessment.
March 6.	Hold kick-off meeting and conduct facility walk-through.
March 13.	Complete Worksheet 1, Worksheet 2 and process flow diagram.
March 20.	Brainstorm opportunities and review for potential.
April 10.	Complete opportunity analysis and Worksheets 3.
April 17.	Review opportunities and complete Worksheets 4 and 5.
May 1.	Completed P2OA report and present to business.

Collect Information

Chapter 3

Get Started	Collect Information	Brainstorm	Analyze	Make Recommendation	Document

1. *Understand chemical, energy, and water use.*
2. *Determine how much waste is being generated and energy is being used.*
3. *Document the scope of the assessment.*
4. *Research similar pollution prevention successes.*
5. *Complete a walkthrough of the assessment area.*

Now that you have committed to performing an assessment, obtained funding, have brought together a team, enlisted management support, and set a schedule, the next step is to start collecting and documenting the information needed to perform the assessment.

The process of gathering data is important but is only one of the beginning steps. The challenge is to gather enough information so that you have a good understanding of the organization's activities that use resources and generate waste without making the task overwhelming by putting too much emphasis on data collection. No more than one-third of the time spent on the assessment should be spent in the data collection step.

The type of information collected depends on the scope of the assessment; where you find the information depends on the data systems already in existence within the organization.

Understand Chemical, Energy, and Water Use

This task involves understanding what chemicals and materials are being used, how much energy is being consumed, and how they are being used. Many chemicals and processes may be available that are less hazardous or generate less waste volume. However, these substitutes may or may not be appropriate for the type of work being performed. Therefore, this task cannot be performed in a vacuum. It involves checking chemical purchasing lists and chemical inventories, but must also involve talking with the staff to understand if they have special requirements, restrictions, or specifications associated with their work that require the use of certain chemicals.

First, gain a general understanding of the chemicals being used. To do this, review chemical inventory lists and chemical purchases. Once you have a general view of the chemicals, talk with staff to understand how the chemicals are being used. This information can be obtained in a variety of ways, ranging from conducting informal conversations to supplying a survey to each of the staff. The following sample questions address the reasons for a staff member's use of particular chemicals:

1. Identify the repeating processes performed in your work area.
   a. What chemicals are needed to perform these processes?
   b. What kind of and how much waste do these processes generate?
2. Identify any upcoming or current one-time processes that are likely to generate a large quantity of waste.
   a. What chemicals are needed to perform these processes?
   b. What kind of and how much waste do these processes generate?

3. Identify the processes that generate the largest volumes of waste.
   a. What chemicals are needed to perform these processes?
   b. What kinds of and how much waste do these processes generate?
4. Identify chemicals that are used because of process requirements or customer specifications.
5. Identify chemicals or processes for which you would like to find alternatives.

To understand energy and water use it is helpful to get copies of a year's (or more) worth of utility bills and any sub-meter data, if available. The utility bills typically offer a facility-wide value that can be analyzed to understand what energy and water use is seasonal versus base load. In most locations the weather is milder in the spring and fall months, which can help identify what portion of the energy use is used for heating and cooling systems versus other building activities. To identify potential energy use reduction opportunities it is useful to look for equipment that typically uses high quantities of energy such as data centers, medical equipment, or organization specific processes.

For water use the first step is to understand where water is being used. In some buildings water is used as part of the building cooling or air conditioning system. Water can also be used for landscape irrigation, ice makers, washing stations, or organization specific processes.

Determine How Much Waste is Being Generated and Energy is Being Used

The next step is to determine waste generation quantities and sources. This will help focus the assessment on the activities that are causing the largest impact on operations. Connecting the chemical use to the waste generation provides the level of detail necessary to refine the scope of the assessment. It allows you to focus on the items that will have the greatest impact. Most organizations have tracking systems for their regulated waste disposal that can be searched for these kinds of data. Other data sources include the staff who manage waste collection and disposal.

Communicating with the staff on their waste generation and gathering information about chemical use can be done simultaneously. The following sample questions address waste generation qualities, quantities, and sources:

1. Identify the largest waste streams over a given period of time.
   a. Are the waste streams generated from multiple processes or just one?
   b. Are the waste streams sanitary, hazardous, or wastewater?

2. Identify problem waste streams, i.e., those that are difficult to dispose of or challenging to manage, or that pose a high risk to staff or the organization.
3. Identify waste streams that may be treatable.

Document the Scope of the Assessment

Now that you have evaluated the chemical use, water use, energy use, and waste generation, refine the scope of the assessment and document it in the assessment worksheets. First, write a detailed scope statement in Worksheet 1 that includes:

- Background information about the group participating in the assessment.
- General description of the work activities and waste being generated.
- Any additional information on the scope of the assessment.
- Areas that are not being included in the assessment and why.
- A list of previously accomplished pollution prevention successes.

Next, document the chemical, energy, and water use and waste generation data gathered in Worksheet 2. Provide these data at the level of detail that is most useful to the assessment; yet be as complete as possible to document the process. If you do not have exact values, use ranges of estimates within an order of magnitude.

See Chapter 7 for specific instructions on each of the worksheets and the appendix for an example of completed worksheets.

Research Similar Pollution Prevention Successes

Now that you have refined the scope of the assessment and know the processes, chemicals, and waste streams that you want to focus on, determine if anyone has previously investigated these same or similar processes. Keep in mind that the technologies for "green" processes have been improving dramatically over the last few years. A technique, technology, or substitute chemical that was tried several years ago may have improved and be worth trying again.

To find this information, seek internal resources first: e.g., your pollution prevention program or specialists, environmental compliance or waste management experts, and other staff performing similar tasks. Some form of reduced scale operations may have already been tested within your organization and you can learn from past experiences. The pollution prevention program may be able to provide copies of past assessments that include similar processes or equipment. The environmental compliance and waste management experts can provide their knowledge of techniques or technologies being used in other, similar organizations. Other staff are excellent resources for understanding the benefits and challenges of a new technique or technology.

Next, look externally. This includes searching the Internet, looking through technical journals and equipment catalogs, and discussing the topic at professional society meetings or websites. These external resources may provide information on ways that other organizations minimize waste generation. Reviewing equipment catalogs for items that are being advertised as "microscale," "environmentally friendly," or "the latest technology" may provide technical solutions to waste generating processes. At the same time, carefully and critically review the information gathered from the Internet, technical journals and equipment catalogs. The technique or technology may be marketed as "environmental" when it is only marginally so, and it might not be applicable to the type of work that you perform.

Complete a Walkthrough of the Assessment Area

The walkthrough of the facility spaces involved in the assessment is the beginning of the creative portion of the assessment process. The intent of the walkthrough is to have the team physically observe all of the facility space(s) that are part of the assessment scope. Seeing where the work is being done and how it is done helps the team place their recommendations in the context of the staff who perform the work. The assessment team's walkthrough also helps to identify additional issues that the team leader could not uncover through the review of chemical, energy, and water use and waste generation.

The walkthrough involves the team leader or facility manager giving a tour of the facility spaces included in the scope of the assessment. The team leader or facility manager coordinates the tour with the staff in the facility spaces so that they expect visitors and understand the purpose of the visit.

The assessment team and the staff should be aware that this walkthrough is *not* an audit but more of a self-assessment. It is vital that the assessment team does not go into the walkthrough with an "auditing attitude." The questions from the assessment team should not be judgments on how the work is currently being done. The team must assume that the staff know best and that they are working diligently to perform the best work that they can. The walkthrough should help the assessment team understand the work and identify any opportunities for pollution prevention. With the assessment team focused on pollution prevention, it will be able to identify new ideas that might be feasible substitutions for current approaches in addition to opportunities that the staff have wanted to pursue but lacked the resources to do so. The following are examples of simple questions that can be useful in understanding the organization's work and identifying potential waste reduction opportunities during a walkthrough:

1. What is this piece of equipment used for?
2. What resources are used and what are they used for?
3. Do you know of any substitutions for this chemical that are less hazardous?
4. Does this activity have to be performed at this scale or could it be smaller?
5. What is in this container, drum, etc.?
6. Why do you do it that way?
7. How do you think you could minimize this waste stream?
8. Can this be reused?

The assessment team needs to listen to the restrictions or reservations the staff have in responding to these questions. They may have specific requirements to meet for the activity or may have tried to change the process in the past. Listen for the difference between real limitations and the feeling that "This is the way we have always done it." If pollution prevention opportunities are identified for people who are not currently on the assessment team, it is important to include them in the remainder of the assessment process so that they can provide input and own any suggestions made to improve their process.

The team should also look at the following areas: secondary activities related to the scope, such as maintenance and washing of equipment; ancillary waste streams, such as pipette tips, glassware, batteries, and rags; non-chemical waste streams, including air emissions and wastewater; and use of raw materials such as water and energy.

Example

The assessment team for the Animal Hospital focused on the materials, energy, and wastes for all the activities in the facility. Priority waste, energy streams, and activities of the Animal Hospital were assessed through staff interviews and procurement records from the bookkeeper. While total energy use was obtained from billing records, energy use by process was calculated based on the number of types of light fixtures and the ratings and hours of use of key pieces of equipment, such as the x-ray machine. The service vendor of the x-ray machines also provided information on use of fixer and the amount of spent chemical waste.

In addition to the interviews and collected documentation, the team conducted several walkthroughs of the Animal Hospital facilities to identify any previously unnoticed waste streams. This information was summarized on the pollution prevention opportunity assessment worksheets. Copies of these can be found in the appendix.

Brainstorm
Chapter 4

Get Started | Collect Information | Brainstorm | Analyze | Make Recommendation | Document

     Implement

1. *Invite the participants.*
2. *Prepare the participants.*
3. *Conduct a brainstorm session.*
4. *Select opportunities.*
5. *Assign actions.*

Now that you have collected and documented information about the organization's operations, you can begin the most creative portion of the assessment: brainstorming opportunities. Brainstorming is a process of creativity followed by action. The essential steps include inviting and preparing the participants, holding the brainstorming session itself, and then assigning actions.

Invite the Participants

At a minimum, the invitation list for the brainstorming session should include the team members. In addition to the team members, invite others who may have useful knowledge of the organization's activities to be involved in the assessment. Make sure that those directly involved in the activity you are reviewing will be in attendance, since they have the best knowledge of the activity and of what others in their field may be doing. Also, it is useful to include experts in other fields in order to bring in new viewpoints.

Prepare the Participants

For the brainstorming session to be effective, those involved need to be well informed about the activity. Send out the activity description, chemical use, and waste generation information that you have collected in advance.

One technique that works well for busy groups is to conduct the walkthrough (as described in Chapter 3) with the core team immediately before the brainstorming session. Devoting a block of time to the assessment, such as two hours for the walkthrough and two hours for the brainstorming and planning session, helps everyone focus on the assessment while the information they have is still fresh in their minds. A walkthrough or data collection effort a few days or even a week ahead can also work well, giving ideas time to develop.

Conduct a Brainstorm Session

The goal of the brainstorming session is to create a list of ideas to reduce material use, reduce waste, and save money. Determining if an idea is practical or possible is done later during the analysis phase. The brainstorming session should be a free flow of ideas and solutions. Bring all the information collected thus far about the organization's activities to the brainstorming meeting, including waste streams, material use, and activity description.

One person should act as the facilitator, recording the ideas being generated. The facilitator guides the meeting to make sure the focus is on source reduction and recycling and reusing materials. The facilitator also makes sure that the group considers all the waste streams involved. The pollution prevention specialist may be a good choice for the facilitator if they are familiar with the organization's operations. Facilitators who are not directly involved in the work are more likely to pose basic questions that no one in the organization has thought to ask, such as, "Why do you do it that way?" or "Why do you do that at all?" Familiarity with processes can make it difficult to see what a pollution prevention specialist may see as a solution or option.

Keeping the brainstorming session focused on pollution prevention is important so that the team can make progress. However, thoughts need to be free, letting the conversation flow so that creativity is encouraged. No ideas are considered silly. The goal of the brainstorming session is to get as many potential pollution prevention ideas contemplated as time allows. Reserve judgment on the feasibility of an idea until all the ideas are verbalized.

As the group discusses each waste stream, the facilitator develops a list of possible opportunities to reduce waste and material use. Even general ideas are useful at this stage because details will be worked out later in the analysis phase.

Select Opportunities

Once the team has developed the ideas and the facilitator has recorded them, the next step is to review and sort the list. Some ideas may be obviously impractical and should be rejected from further study. Other ideas may be so similar that they can be combined into a single item. The focus can also be placed on opportunities that reduce more difficult or hazardous waste streams. Narrow the list down to a reasonable number, about 3 to 10 workable ideas (pollution prevention opportunities). For further investigation, gather more information about each idea and analyze the information.

Prepare a list of the pollution prevention opportunities that were not pursued and make note as to why they were not considered at this time. This list is included in the documentation on Worksheet 4 and offers useful information regarding potential future pollution prevention opportunities that may be considered during continuous improvement efforts that occur after the assessment. This list may also provide a starting point for any future assessments that might be performed by identifying options that might be worth pursuing and items that were determined impractical or technically infeasible and therefore not worth further investigation.

Assign Actions

Assigning the investigation of each workable pollution prevention opportunity is crucial. The analysis of these opportunities is the most time-consuming and important part of the pollution prevention opportunity assessment. The team leader either assigns these jobs to team members or takes on responsibility for most of the analysis and assigns the information gathering tasks to others. Ideally, before the brainstorming meeting ends or soon after, the team leader should have assigned each opportunity to a person who is responsible for its investigation. The team will then leave with actions to accomplish as the next phase of the assessment.

 ## Example

The brainstorming session for the Animal Hospital took place a week after the walkthrough. The team leader used the time between the walkthrough and the brainstorming session to document and summarize the information from the walkthrough and related interviews. The brainstorming session was done both in-person with the staff as well as through online consultation with other pollution prevention experts. Together, they generated about 11 major opportunities. The team leader working with owner then prioritized the opportunities, grouping some together, rejecting some as not worth further study, and highlighting those that could be valuable. This resulted in four opportunities for further analysis:

- Retrofitting florescent light fixtures with LED bulbs.
- Purchasing a digital x-ray machine.
- Purchasing of biodegradable laundry soap.
- Purchasing recycled paper products and use of duplexing.

The assessment team leader then carefully planned out the additional data collection and research needed to fully document and assess each opportunity. She communicated the additional data needs to the rest of the team, who provided assistance.

Analyze
Chapter 5

Get Started   **Collect Information**   **Brainstorm**   **Analyze**   **Make Recommendation**   **Document**

Implement

1. *Describe the opportunities.*
2. *Perform a qualitative analysis.*
3. *Perform a quantitative analysis.*
4. *Determine the amount of waste reduced and energy saved.*
5. *Evaluate cost avoidance.*
6. *Determine implementation cost.*
7. *Calculate payback.*
8. *Calculate return-on-investment.*

With brainstorming and prioritization complete, you now have a selection of potential waste reducing opportunities that may save money for your organization. To determine if these ideas are worth implementing, you need to conduct an analysis of each opportunity, preferably both qualitative and quantitative analyses.

Describe the Opportunities

The analysis of the pollution prevention opportunities begins with writing out the opportunities in detail. In the worksheets provided in Chapter 7, a description of the current practice is used to define the activity. Next, the pollution prevention opportunity is described as the proposed action to replace the current practice. This includes a qualitative description of the expected benefits and any challenges that may arise. The purpose of documenting the current practice and recommended action is to provide enough detail to solicit implementation funding, if needed, and to explain the opportunities analyzed to those who read the assessment.

Perform a Qualitative Analysis

Some form of qualitative and quantitative analyses will need to be performed for both the current practices and the recommended actions. The following steps can help develop the qualitative analysis:

1. Determine what would be required to implement this opportunity, such as buying new equipment or supplies, conducting new operations, or writing a new procedure.
2. If you will need to buy equipment, contact vendors to determine what equipment is needed, its specifications and efficiency, energy and materials use, ancillary equipment or software required, implementation requirements, and cost. Talk to several vendors to get a range of options and requirements.
3. Determine how much labor or training will be required to install and use the new equipment.
4. If you are doing a procedure or process change, determine who will be developing and who will be using the new method, what materials are needed and their costs, how many hours are needed to develop or research the new method, and training needed to implement the new method.
5. Evaluate and document other benefits besides waste, energy, and cost reduction, such as increased safety, reduced worker exposure, improved

operations capacity, higher quality products, marketability of an innovative technique, and any others.

Perform a Quantitative Analysis

The quantitative analysis evaluates the potential waste reduction, energy savings, and cost savings. It should answer four essential questions:

1. How much waste and energy use will the opportunity reduce, either annually or one-time?
2. How much money will the opportunity save, either annually or one-time?
3. What will be the up-front cost to implement the waste and energy use reduction measures?
4. What will be the payback or the return-on-investment?

Determine Amounts of Waste Reduced and Energy Saved

There are two kinds of waste reduction: annual and one-time reductions. Annual reductions come from changing an ongoing process so that savings will be yielded for many years after the new technology or technique has been implemented. An example of an annual reduction is changing an analytical process from full-scale to microscale for all future analysis. One-time savings come from making changes to a single action, such as sending excess chemicals from an inventory reduction to another, similar organization for reuse, instead of disposal.

To determine the amount of waste that will be reduced from each opportunity, the following steps should be taken:

1. Review the amount of waste generated now (from a routine process) or estimate the amount of waste to be generated from a one-time activity.
2. Estimate how much waste will be reduced from each pollution prevention opportunity, based on the information gathered when developing the pollution prevention idea. The reduction may be based on efficiency of new equipment, percent reduction in the amount of materials required, or amount of materials recycled or reused.
3. Determine what type of waste will be reduced, as this can greatly impact costs. Waste is usually either hazardous (sent to a qualified hazardous waste disposal company) or nonhazardous (sent to a sanitary landfill or sanitary sewer). Hazardous waste is much more expensive and time-consuming to dispose of than nonhazardous waste. The waste form is also important: solid waste (including liquids that are lab-packed, that is,

packaged as a solid waste), liquid waste going to a process or sanitary sewer, and gaseous air emissions.

4. Determine which wastes will be eliminated or reduced, as well as any reductions in the toxicity of a waste (such as reducing hazardous waste to nonhazardous waste).

Energy use reduction is similar, although most energy saving actions result in annual, not one-time, savings. The analysis steps are also similar:

1. Review the amount of energy used now. This can be done using utility and purchase statements (electricity, gas, fuel) and through calculations based on the hours used and demand from equipment and lighting. Ideally, both these methods are used to validate energy demand from two methods.
2. Estimate how much energy will be saved from each pollution prevention opportunity, based on the information gathered when developing the idea. Be sure to validate the calculations by comparing them as a percentage to the total energy demand.
3. Consider the source of energy and upstream pollution. In addition to reducing energy demand, energy related opportunities can include converting to a cleaner form of energy, such as installing solar panels at the facility site or converting to electric vehicles.

Evaluate Cost Avoidance

Total cost avoidance comes from four types of savings:

$$Cost\ avoidance = \begin{array}{l} waste\ disposal\ savings + energy\ use\ reduction\ savings \\ + raw\ material\ purchase\ savings + labor\ savings \end{array}$$

Waste disposal savings - the amount of waste reduced, multiplied by the unit cost of disposing of those wastes. Waste disposal savings should include the cost to collect, log, handle, package, and ship the waste.

Energy use reduction savings – the amount of energy reduced, multiplied by the unit cost of energy, which can include demand charges.

Raw material purchase savings - the amount of new materials you would avoid having to purchase because of reuse or reduced use, multiplied by their unit costs.

Labor savings - the amount of labor time reduced, multiplied by a unit labor rate. Labor savings can arise from process efficiencies from new equipment or methods, reduced time spent ordering materials or maintaining equipment, and reduced compliance and safety requirements.

An easy way to estimate savings is to use the cost items listed above to calculate the cost before the opportunity and the cost after the opportunity, then subtract them:

$$\text{Cost avoidance} = \begin{array}{l} \textit{total costs before opportunity} \\ - \textit{estimated total costs after implementation} \end{array}$$

Determine Implementation Cost

Implementation cost is the one-time expense to make the change to the process. Implementation cost comes from two types of expenses:

$$\textit{Implementation cost} = \textit{equipment purchase costs} + \textit{labor costs for implementation}$$

Equipment purchase costs - the costs paid to the vendors to buy new equipment, plus any software or ancillary equipment, taxes, purchase adders, or additional direct costs.

Labor costs for implementation - the number of hours required to implement the new activity, multiplied by a labor rate. Labor costs for implementation include costs for development of a new method or process, changing permits or other regulatory permissions, selecting and installing equipment, training, writing new procedures, and providing any reports required for start-up.

Evaluate Payback

The final analysis step is to determine if it is financially worthwhile to implement a waste reduction project.

For projects with *annual savings*, the simplest kind of cost analysis is simple payback:

$$\textit{payback (years)} = \frac{\textit{implementation cost (\$)}}{\textit{annual cost avoidance (\$/year)}}$$

The payback is the number of years or the fraction of the year needed to repay the initial investment in implementing the opportunity. Most businesses consider projects with up to a three-year payback worthwhile to implement. However, some businesses look only at one-year paybacks, while others think more long-term, for instance, up to ten-year paybacks.

For projects having *one-time savings*, subtract the implementation cost from the one-time savings:

$$payback\ (\$) = cost\ avoidance\ (\$) - implementation\ costs\ (\$)$$

If the result is positive (> zero), it is worthwhile to implement.

Evaluate Return on Investment (ROI)

Businesses that use a percent return on investment measurement often require at least a 33% ROI, though some require as much as a 100% return and others as low as 10%.

To calculate ROI, inverse the payback calculation and multiply by 100 to get a percentage:

$$\%\ ROI = [annual\ costs\ savings\ (\$/year)\ /\ implementation\ costs\ (\$)]\ x\ 100$$

If you want to take into account the time-cost of money or depreciation, the calculation becomes a little more complex. Here is one way to calculate it:

$$\%\ ROI/year = \frac{annual\ cost\ savings\ (\$/year) - \dfrac{Implementation\ costs\ (\$)}{life\ of\ project\ (years)}}{Implementation\ cost\ (\$)}\ x\ 100$$

The *life of project* is how long the new equipment or new process will be used, usually 5 to 20 years.

For most small to medium sized businesses and for opportunities with minimal capital costs, simple payback calculations are usually sufficient.

Example

A detailed analysis was conducted on four opportunities developed during the brainstorming session for the Animal Hospital. The analysis of the first opportunity is summarized in the following example. The analysis for all the opportunities is included in the appendix.

Opportunity

Purchase of a digital x-ray machine.

Current Practice

The Animal Hospital processes x-rays for domestic animals using a Konica Medical Processor film machine. The clinic processes about 400 images a year using this equipment. The machine requires supplies and a monthly service call for calibration and cleaning. Additionally, the film processing requires developer and fixer chemicals that are disposed of as wastewater once a month. Residual silver remaining in the developer/fixer solution, resulting from the film processing, is not recovered from these chemicals during disposal.

Proposed Action

The recommended action is to replace the film x-ray machine with a digital x-ray machine. This action would decrease energy costs, waste disposal, labor costs, toxic silver disposal, and environmental impacts. Additional benefits include better patient care as digital images go directly to a patient's file and reduced x-ray exposure resulting from occasional retakes of ineffective x-rays. Digital images can be manipulated for contrast, exposure, and enlargements. The dark room currently used for film processing and storage space needed for film x-ray processing could be used for other purposes. Service calls would reduce from monthly to approximately every 2 years.

Calculation of Waste Reduction and Energy Savings

The Animal Hospital currently uses approximately 3,432 kWh per year of electricity for the x-ray machine. The digital machine would use about 8 kWh per year, resulting in a savings of 3,424 kWh per year. The digital machine would also eliminate about 60 gal per year of waste solution (containing silver) from the x-ray film developer/fixer.

Calculation of Annual Cost Savings

Current

Electricity (at $0.10/kWh)	$343
X-ray supplies	$600
Service contract ($75/month)	$900
Labor to process the film (5 mins/image)	$400
Total	$2243

Proposed

Electricity (at $0.10/kWh)	$1
X-ray supplies (eliminated)	$0
Service contract (minimal)	$0
Labor to process the film (eliminated)	$0
Total	$1

Annual Cost Savings: $2243 - $1 = $2242

Calculation of Implementation Cost and Payback

Implementation Cost

Digital x-ray machine	$17,250
Labor for installation and training	$250
Total	$17,500

Payback (Implementation Costs/Annual Cost Savings)   :$17,500/$2242 = 7.8 years

Recommend
Chapter 6

Get Started	Collect Information	Brainstorm	Analyze	Make Recommendation	Document

1. *Select opportunities for implementation.*
2. *Document the implementation strategy.*
3. *Present results to management.*
4. *Implement recommended opportunities.*

Now that the team has identified and researched the pollution prevention opportunities relevant to organization's operations, the next action is to decide which of these should be implemented. This step in the assessment leads into implementation, the most important activity that follows an assessment. Pollution prevention opportunity assessments provide the technical and cost savings basis for recommending changes to an organization's techniques or equipment. This section discusses how to consolidate the information that has been collected and use it to garner implementation resources. Implementing the pollution prevention opportunities identified in the assessment is a crucial step in the culture change that begins once staff find that preventing pollution provides opportunities to advance their operational capabilities.

Select Opportunities for Implementation

In order to select opportunities to implement, first review the payback calculated for each. Consider first those opportunities that have little or no implementation cost associated with them. Next, any opportunity that has a payback of three years or less as usually worth considering for implementation. Items with a payback period longer than three years may be worth implementing as well, depending on other benefits. Reasons to implement opportunities regardless of payback include: impact on a high-profile activity, reduction of a high volume of waste, reduction of a highly dangerous waste, reduction of risk and liability, reduced worker exposure, simplicity of implementation, high interest by staff member(s), or broad applicability in other parts of the organization.

Document Implementation Strategy

Now that you have researched the pollution prevention opportunities and selected the ones you want to implement, it is time to document the strategy to implement the recommendations. First summarize the numerical results of the opportunities by listing the opportunity title, waste type reduced, annual waste or energy use reduction, estimated annual cost savings, estimated implementation cost, and payback.

Next, summarize the opportunities and document the implementation recommendations identified by the assessment team. This summary should include the identification of opportunities that are not being pursued further and a prioritized list of the opportunities that are considered worthy of implementation. The opportunities that are being considered for implementation need to be organized as follows:

- Opportunities that should be pursued immediately because they are free or very low cost
- Opportunities that should be pursued immediately and the source of the implementation resources
- Strategy for identifying implementation resources for implementation of the remaining opportunities on the list.

See Chapter 7 for specific instructions on each of the worksheets and the appendix for an example of completed worksheets.

Present Results to Management

One of the keys to the success of a pollution prevention program is the involvement of managers or organizational leaders. Communicating the results of a pollution prevention opportunity assessment is one way to share the organization's progress in improving the bottom line as well as demonstrating that staff are proactive in finding solutions to their environmental challenges.

The recommendations of the assessment should be presented to key management and decisionmakers. At this time, provide managers with a list of projects that are going to be implemented because they are easy and inexpensive, show them the effect that these projects have on the bottom line, and provide a list of opportunities that are worthy of being implemented but need implementation resources. Emphasize any improvements to operations, risk reduction, and reduced compliance costs. Demonstrating that you have researched and prioritized the opportunities based on their financial benefit to the company typically provides managers the data they need to justify investment. Additionally, proactively identifying and researching pollution prevention opportunities and showing that you have implemented all of the projects within a budget demonstrates commitment to saving the organization money, improving safety, reducing risk, and investing in the environment.

Implement Recommended Opportunities

As mentioned above, the first opportunities that should be implemented are those that are free or nearly free. The next step is to identify sources of funding for the opportunities that are determined worthy of implementation but do not have the resources to implement. First, consider funding these opportunities with regular operations funds, using the payback information as a selling point to the funding clients of those activities. The next route is to talk with the management of your organization to see if there are internal funds that would support pollution prevention investments. Next, contact your pollution prevention specialists to find out about any implementation programs that might be available. Finally, if internal or client resources are not available, look externally for Federal, state, and local government and other resources that might support pollution prevention implementation projects.

Example

Four pollution prevention opportunities were identified as part of the Animal Hospital assessment. Of these, one had significant chemical waste reduction and energy savings and a second had major energy savings. These were both recommended for implementation due to their acceptable paybacks and significant waste and energy reduction, as well as other benefits for the clinic and its staff. The remaining two opportunities had smaller waste reductions and very small savings or slight increase in annual costs. They were still recommended for implementation because represent good green management practices and are simple to implement at very little to no cost. Overall, the results indicated that if all the opportunities implemented, the annual costs savings for the Animal Hospital would be about $2,400, with an energy savings of almost 5,000 kWh (30% of their annual electricity use), and a reduction of about 70 kg of chemical sewer waste.

Document
Chapter 7

Get
Started

Collect
Information

Brainstorm

Analyze

Make
Recommendation

Document

1. *Complete pollution prevention opportunity worksheets.*
2. *Provide report to management and staff.*

The task often considered the least inspiring—documentation—is also one of the most important. It is important that the assessment be documented *as it is being performed.* The final documentation is the completed worksheets, which become the record of the pollution prevention opportunity assessment. Properly completed, the worksheets summarize the recommended actions, the next steps, and the point-of-contact information in enough detail that the ideas can be implemented.

Additionally, the documentation of one assessment can be used as a beginning for the next assessment in a similar operations area. Occasionally, assessments will identify opportunities that apply not only to a particular operation but also to other operations. Other benefits of good documentation include use of documentation to easily prepare proposals for funding and use of the documentation as evidence of a pollution prevention program for regulators and others.

Complete Pollution Prevention Opportunity Worksheets

The following five worksheets have been found to be useful in documenting the pollution prevention opportunity assessment efforts. The worksheets are outlined below and also provided as complete worksheets with instructions for each section at the end of this chapter. Examples of completed worksheets can be found in the appendix.

Worksheet 1:	*Team and Activity Description* Documents the background and scope of the assessment.
Worksheet 2:	*Activity Flow Diagram* Documents the materials flow and mass balance within the scope of the assessment.
Worksheet 3:	*Pollution Prevention Opportunity* Documents each of the pollution prevention ideas that are being considered for the assessment. There will be one of these worksheets for each idea being analyzed; thus each assessment will have several Worksheets 3 when the assessment is completed.
Worksheet 4:	*Pollution Prevention Opportunities Summary* Summarizes the benefits of the pollution prevention opportunities and lists opportunities that were brainstormed but not included in the assessment.
Worksheet 5:	*Final Summary* Summarizes the recommendations and strategies for implementation of the pollution prevention opportunities identified in the assessment.

Experience has shown that the details provided in a well-documented pollution prevention opportunity assessment can be used in a variety of ways:

- Documenting a comprehensive approach to managing and minimizing waste to regulators, shareholders, and other interested parties
- Providing a methodology (logical steps) for performing future assessments from beginning to end
- Demonstrating the benefits (such as waste reduction, staff time saved, and cost savings) associated with performing assessments
- Communicating pollution prevention opportunities that might be applicable elsewhere in the organization and by similar organizations
- Encouraging other parts of the organization to perform assessments and implement waste reduction opportunities
- Recognizing an organization's success in completing the assessment through publications and awards
- Drafting implementation resource requests.

In addition to the worksheets, many assessment teams include executive summaries to summarize the assessment for management as well as appendices with detailed information supporting the assessment calculations or process.

Provide Report to Management and Staff

Once the worksheets have been completed it is important to share the assessment results with management, the assessment team, and other interested staff. Management needs to be made aware of the completed assessment so they know that you are working toward continuous improvement in your work, avoiding environmental compliance issues by acting proactively, reducing waste at the source, and reducing costs. The assessment team and staff, especially those that will be responsible for implementation and new operations, need the report to see the entire analysis and take action.

Example

The team leader completed the worksheets and prepared an executive summary as part of the P2OA report. The complete document, including worksheets and executive summary, is included in the appendix. She also included an appendix with additional information about the specific vendors that could provide the replacement materials, including their contact information. Particularly important, she included price quotes from several vendors for digital x-ray machines, as well as information on installation, training, and maintenance.

The results were presented to the owner of the Animal Hospital both as a report and a dynamic and illustrated slide presentation.

Pollution Prevention Opportunity Assessment
Worksheet 1
Team and Activity Description

Date: P2OA ID Code: Facility:

Activity: ①

Team Members (*Leader)   Organization   Contact Info

②

Description of Activity to be Examined in this P2OA

③

Worksheet 1 Instructions

The intent of Worksheet 1 is to provide the background and scope of the assessment. See Chapter 2 for direction on how to collect the information needed for Worksheet 1. To complete each section of worksheet 1:

- Identify the date the worksheet was completed or last updated and the facility name.
- Use an identifying (ID) code to organize multiple assessments by an organization.
- Title the activity covered by the assessment (typically named after the organization's name, their building, the division, and/or their type of work).

- Provide the team members' names and contact information.
- Flag the team leader who is the primary point of contact for the assessment.
- Provide brief titles for team members, such as, pollution prevention specialist, operations, owner, etc.

- Provide detailed background information about the organization being assessed, especially information that will be needed for the later analysis (e.g., name of the organization, type of work, number and key roles of staff, number and types of activities conducted, size of building where they are located, etc.).
- Provide overall description of waste generated or activities at the facility.
- Provide scope of assessment (if different than above).
- Provide a list of the areas *not* being considered in this assessment and why (can be general, such as, "no waste streams under 1 kg were considered," or specific, such as, "the Biology department staff also housed in the Chemistry building were not included in the scope of this assessment").
- Provide a list of previously accomplished pollution prevention activities.
- If more detail is available, include one paragraph descriptions of the spaces being assessed and all the processes that are included within the scope.

Pollution Prevention Opportunity Assessment
Worksheet 2
Materials Flow Diagram

Date: P2OA ID Code: Facility:

Activity:

Chemical Inputs	
Name	Qty.

①

Material and Water Inputs	
Name	Qty.

Energy Inputs	
Name	Qty.

②

Activity
Activity Time Period

Product or Result	
Name	Qty.

③

Hazardous Chemical Waste Output	
Name	Qty.

Non-Hazardous Solid Waste Output	
Name	Qty.

Waste Water Output	
Name	Qty.

Air Emissions	
Name	Qty.

Other

Worksheet 2 Instructions

The intent of Worksheet 2 is to demonstrate a materials flow and mass balance within the scope being assessed. A comprehensive mass balance is not always feasible or relevant for pollution prevention opportunity assessments, so it is optional for this worksheet. The input materials and the waste output, including quantities, are the important portions of this worksheet. See Chapter 3 for direction on how to collect the information needed for Worksheet 2. To complete each section of Worksheet 2:

- List and provide quantities of key chemical, materials, water, energy, and other relevant resource inputs being addressed within the scope of the assessment.

- Provide a short description of the work being performed.
- Include the time period that the quantities refer to, typically annually or monthly

- List the product or result of the process, such as the number of items produced or customers served.
- List and provide quantities of key waste streams by type being addressed within the scope of this assessment.

Pollution Prevention Opportunity Assessment
Worksheet 3
Pollution Prevention Opportunity Description

Date: P2OA ID Code: Facility:
Activity:

P2O No.   P2O Title:

Current Practice

Recommended Action

Calculation of Waste Reduction and/or Energy Savings

Calculation of Annual Cost Savings

Calculation of Implementation Cost and Payback

Vendor/Contact Information

Worksheet 3 Instructions

The intent of Worksheet 3 is to document the pollution prevention opportunities that are being considered for the assessment. There should be one Worksheet 3 for every pollution prevention opportunity that is analyzed. Typically, the number of opportunities recorded on Worksheet 3s range from 3 to 10, depending on the scope of the assessment, complexity of the pollution prevention opportunities suggested, and how much pollution prevention was performed previously. See Chapters 4 and 5 for direction on how to collect and calculate the information needed for Worksheet 3. To complete each section of Worksheet 3:

- Uniquely title each pollution prevention opportunity.

- Provide a description of how the current work process and/or activity is being performed, how much waste it is generating, how much and what type of energy it uses, what type of equipment it is using, the amount of staff time required, the types of chemicals used, and what the work is trying to accomplish.

- Describe the proposed pollution prevention action including the details on the changes that would need to be made; what type of equipment would be required (if any); generally whether it would reduce waste, energy use, materials use, time, money, or hazard level; what activities would need to be performed for implementation to take place, etc.
- Describe the actions that will need to be performed for implementation. Provide enough detail and specifications that this opportunity could be implemented by someone reading this description later.

- Describe the waste type being minimized or eliminated and provide the quantity; show all calculations.
- Describe any energy or materials savings and provide quantity; show all calculations.

- Provide detail on both the annual costs of the current practice and the operations cost after proposed opportunity is implemented (not including implementation costs). Show calculations of annual cost savings associated with changing the proposed action. Note that the cost includes the cost of managing and disposing of waste, changes in staff time to perform the work, changes in cost of purchased items, and any other relevant costs that can be identified (see Chapter 5).

- Calculate implementation cost (see Chapter 5).
- Calculate payback (see Chapter 5).

- Provide contact details of any internal or external resources that could be contacted if this opportunity were to be implemented. This may include vendors of equipment, sources of cost quotes, and any experts consulted. Additional information can be included in an appendix.

Pollution Prevention Opportunity Assessment
Worksheet 4
Pollution Prevention Opportunities Summary

Date: P2OA ID Code: Facility:
Activity:

P2O No.	P2O Title	Waste Class Reduced	Annual Waste Reduction or Energy Savings	Estimated Annual Cost Savings	Estimated Implementation Cost	Payback
1						
2						
3						

Other Brainstorming Opportunities Considered but Not Analyzed

Worksheet 4 Instructions

The intent of Worksheet 4 is to summarize the benefits identified in Worksheet 3. This table has no new data in it, just the titles of opportunities, waste types reduced, waste and energy use reduction, cost savings, implementation cost, and payback information calculated on Worksheet 3. The only new information on this worksheet is a list of brainstorming opportunities that were not pursued and an explanation of why they were not considered at this time. To complete each section of Worksheet 4:

- Copy the title of each opportunity into one row each of the table.

- Copy the waste type reduced, waste reduction quantity, cost savings and payback final calculations into the appropriate columns.

- List any opportunities that were discussed in your brainstorming session but were not analyzed. Provide a reason why they were not pursued at this time (this helps document any ideas you ruled out for others reading your assessment in the future).

Pollution Prevention Opportunity Assessment
Worksheet 5
Final Summary

Date: P2OA ID Code: Facility:

Activity:

Proposed Opportunities and Discussion

①

Recommendations and Schedule for Implementation

②

Worksheet 5 Instructions

The intent of Worksheet 5 is to provide recommendations for implementation and a strategy for implementing and/or identifying resources needed to implement. See Chapter 6 for direction on how to collect the information needed for Worksheet 5. To complete each section of Worksheet 5:

- Briefly summarize and discuss the benefits and challenges of the pollution prevention opportunities (on Worksheet 3) that were evaluated.

- Summarize the opportunities that are recommended for implementation and why. Describe the steps that should be taken to implement each recommended opportunity. Mention any opportunities that were recommended and already implemented during the assessment.
- Briefly summarize the opportunities that are recommended for implementation but need funding/resources from a source external to the team. Describe the recommended path forward for pursuing implementation funds. Identify point of contact for the implementation of this opportunity.
- Briefly summarize the opportunities that are marginally recommended for implementation, explain why they are only marginal, and describe the best path forward as it is seen now. Also, provide a date to re-evaluate those opportunities to see if their chances of implementation improve over time.
- Describe any assessed opportunities that are not recommended and why (e.g., poor ROI, not feasible, etc.)
- Optional – Provide 'lessons learned' on the assessment that can be used as recommendations to the pollution prevention specialist on the next assessment.

Conclusion
Chapter 8

Completing a pollution prevention opportunity assessment is both a first step towards preventing waste and an essential part of a complete pollution prevention program. An assessment can be conducted at a grassroots level, with staff and pollution prevention specialists diving into their work processes, developing creative techniques, and finding new technologies to reduce their waste streams. By combining assessments with a complete pollution prevention program, you can build a strong environmental management system and the beginnings of an environmental culture change within an organization.

Ultimately, conducting formal pollution prevention opportunity assessments gives structure to a creative analytical process and formalizes an environmental consciousness that most staff have by nature and by training. It provides the time, resources, and framework for staff to create ideas, conduct analyses, and make recommendations to reduce waste. By implementing these recommendations, they can improve their processes in a way that is useful to customers, managers, regulators, and themselves. Assessments make the process of reducing chemical and material use and taking a step towards long-term reduced environmental impact both achievable and desirable.

Example

When the team completed and presented the assessment of the Animal Hospital, the owner expressed keen interest in all the opportunities. He and his staff were particularly surprised at the energy use and the annual cost of the x-ray machine. They had understood the chemical use and monthly maintenance, but were surprised that it represented a major part of their electricity bill as well. Although it will take over 7 years to payback the new purchase, the reduction in chemical waste, energy use, and worker exposure to those chemicals represented a big enough benefit that they have purchased a digital x-ray machine, as well as implemented all the other opportunities.

Involvement in the pollution prevention opportunity assessment led the Animal Hospital to a new way of thinking and was the incentive for them to take action. They now consider new approaches rather than the status quo. Pollution prevention has helped make the Animal Hospital a more competitive small business.

Definitions &
Acronyms
Appendix 1

Implementation cost: the one-time expense involved in making the change to your process

Payback: the length of time for cost avoidance to equal the investment cost of a project

Pollution prevention: reduction of waste through source reduction and recycling/reuse

Pollution prevention opportunity assessment: a systematic, documented approach to determining where pollution prevention opportunities exist and the best methods to implement those opportunities

Return-on-investment (ROI): the percent of the annual savings of the total investment cost

Reuse/Recycling: reusing chemicals and materials, or reprocessing or recycling instead of disposing of them

Source reduction: reducing waste at the source before it is generated

Treatment: reducing the toxicity or volume of waste before safely disposing of it

Example
Appendix 2

Pollution Prevention Opportunity Assessment[1]

P2OA-2014-01

Animal Hospital

1 May 2014

[1] **NOTE: This P2OA was prepared from real-life P2OAs for veterinary clinics conducted by a graduate engineering student. Identifying information has been removed and permission was received from both the student and the business to adapt their assessment as a generic example.**

Executive Summary

This Pollution Prevention Opportunity Assessment (P2OA) is for the Animal Hospital, a small clinic that provides routine and emergency care for domestic animals. The team for this project consisted of pollution prevention experts and the owner of the business and its staff. This assessment was done in phases, utilizing collaboration with other team members.

The assessment began on February 24, 2014 with planning completed on March 3. The first site visit was on March 6. During that visit, a walk-through was conducted and information about processes collected through staff interviews with office manager and vet technicians. Possible pollution prevention opportunities were recorded, with the focus on the Animal Hospital and its clinic only. The course of action was to assess increasing energy efficiency and reduced toxicity for the facility.

Recommendations from staff included a digital x-ray machine and assessment of better lighting. A second site visit was performed on March 10, 2014 to obtain purchasing and energy records, as well as to brainstorm ideas. A third site visit on April 17 included discussion of final assessments and strategies for feasible opportunities. Results for this P2OA are summarized below and detailed in the following pages.

The team identified eleven pollution prevention opportunities for consideration of which four were chosen for evaluation. These four opportunities had the greatest impact for long-term pollution prevention and reduced environmental impacts. If all four opportunities in this report were implemented, the Animal Hospital would realize an annual energy use reduction of 4994 kWh (almost 30% of the clinic's annual energy use), sanitary waste reduction of about 70 kg, and an annual cost savings of $2,369. Through research of environmentally preferable opportunities, additional cost saving might be realized with commercial business tax deductions and credits.

The first opportunity was to reduce energy use for the lighting needed for day-to-day operations at the clinic. Ten of the 16 fixtures are illuminated over ten hours per day. It was determined that by retrofitting the 16 existing fluorescent light fixtures with LED light tubes a reduction of 47% energy use could be obtained. This opportunity results in an annual cost savings of $166. It is recommended that this be implemented.

The second opportunity assessed the replacement of the film x-ray machine with a digital x-ray machine. The clinic does about 400 film x-ray's per year requiring chemical developer, fixer and a dark room to be used for processing. The chemical waste solution is disposed of into the sewer system monthly by a service technician when he calibrates the machine. During processing of the x-ray film, silver by-products are deposited in the chemical waste solution. Studies have found that 1.1g/L of silver can be recovered from the chemical waste. Silver is highly toxic to the environment and a finite natural resource that is in limited quantities. The chemical waste can be recycled but considering other pollution and high cost factors associated with film x-rays, it is the team's suggestion to switch to digital x-rays. A 99.8% reduction in energy use can be achieved, resulting in 3,424 kWh saved per year. Annual cost savings of $2,242 per year makes this a highly desirable opportunity to implement.

The third opportunity involves substituting currently used laundry soap with a concentrated plant based, environmentally friendly detergent. Most laundry soaps contain petroleum-based ingredients that are not biodegradable and harmful to the environment. The Animal Hospital averages 15 loads of laundry per week, creating a lot of wastewater pollution. Plant-based products are readily available in stores including where the Animal Hospital shops. For example, "Ecos Plus" detergent does not contain 1,4-Dioxane, a known carcinogen. This opportunity would save $18/year and reduce consumption of a 14.7kg bucket of laundry soap. This opportunity is an easy, cost efficient and environmentally beneficial opportunity to pursue.

The Animal Hospital uses about 20,000 sheets (40 reams) of copier paper per year. Currently they use non-recycled paper. The final opportunity involves switching their current 0% post-consumer waste (PCW) copier paper to 100% PCW recycled paper. Additional savings can be obtained by utilizing the duplexing feature for document printing of receipts and records. Duplexing could save over 3,000 sheets per year with a cost savings of $19. The cost of 100% PCW recycled copier paper is slightly higher ($5.99/ream) than the 0% currently used by the Animal Hospital ($3.19/ream) but this opportunity should still be considered as unrealized environment savings, like reduced tree cutting for virgin paper, achieves pollution prevention goals.

```
┌─────────────────────────────────────────────────────────────────┐
│              Pollution Prevention Opportunity Assessment          │
│                             Worksheet 1                           │
│                    Team and Activity Description                  │
│                                                                   │
│ Date: May 1, 2014  P2OA ID Code: P2OA-2014-01  Facility: Animal   │
│ Hospital                                                          │
│                                                                   │
│ Activity: Veterinarian services of domestic animals              │
└─────────────────────────────────────────────────────────────────┘
```

Team Members (*Leader)	Organization	Contact Info
Ms. S. Penn*	P2 Experts	
Dr. J. Engel-Cox	P2 Experts	
Dr. G. Vett	Animal Hospital	
Ms. O. Mann	Animal Hospital	

Description of Activity to be Examined in This P2OA

This Pollution Prevention assessment evaluated all activities at the Animal Hospital, located in Any Town, Any Country. This facility is a local animal hospital that provides routine and emergency care for domestic animals. Services include vaccinations, onsite routine blood laboratory testing, x-rays, chemotherapy, special dietary needs, geriatric care, emergency care, surgeries such as spay/neuter, infection/abscess treatments, dental cleaning, and doctor house calls. The facility has a staff of 8 professional personnel consisting of one veterinary physician, one office manager, one receptionist and 5 support/ veterinary assistants. All work is performed onsite, Monday – Friday (except doctor house calls) including routine laboratory work. All onsite activities were examined in this P2OA.

Priority streams and activities of the Animal Hospital were assessed through staff interviews and procurement records from the bookkeeper. This facility sees approximately 140+ patients per week with surgeries/dental cleanings conducted about 3 days per week. The vet clinic consists of a waiting room, 3 examination rooms, 1 office, 1 supply storage room, 1 technician area/hallway, 1 x-ray room, 1 dark room/storage, 1 kennel/recovery room for animals, 1 surgical room, and a laundry/bathroom area. Laboratory equipment to perform routine blood and urine tests are located in an adjacent office space, which is shared with another company (lab area was not assessed). Light fixtures include incandescent lights in two areas, laundry/bathroom, and dark room/storage areas, each having one 60-watt incandescent light bulb. All other lighting fixtures at the Animal Hospital are fluorescent lighting located in a drop tile ceiling. There are 14 large and 2 small multidirectional fluorescent tube units. This assessment will evaluate conversion of the fluorescent tube lights with high efficiency LED lighting.

The Animal Hospital currently images and processes approximately 5 x-rays per week utilizing a Konica Medical Film Processor SRX-101A. The x-ray machine requires onsite mixing of developer, tap water, and fixer chemicals for the developing process; additionally, film developing must be done in a designated dark room. The clinic has a monthly service contract, where a technician calibrates and disposes of the spent, liquid chemical waste solution from the developing process. This spent, liquid chemical waste is poured into the sewer system. The film and developer contain trace amounts of silver but due to the Animal Hospital's low x-ray volume there is no silver recovery unit installed on the machine.

The Animal Hospital currently does limited recycling consisting of reuse of medical prescription bottles donated by patients. They also repurpose empty vaccine trays as urine catch basins. They do not recycle cardboard or office paper at this time. Surgical machinery and appliances were utilized in an efficient manner so they were not assessed. There is a limited amount of expired medications or unused chemotherapy supplies which were either donated or disposed of properly. The surgical room has an onsite autoclave machine for sterilization so no unnecessary waste is generated in the surgical room process.

Following is a process flow diagram of the Animal Hospital's major activities, energy and material inputs, and waste streams.

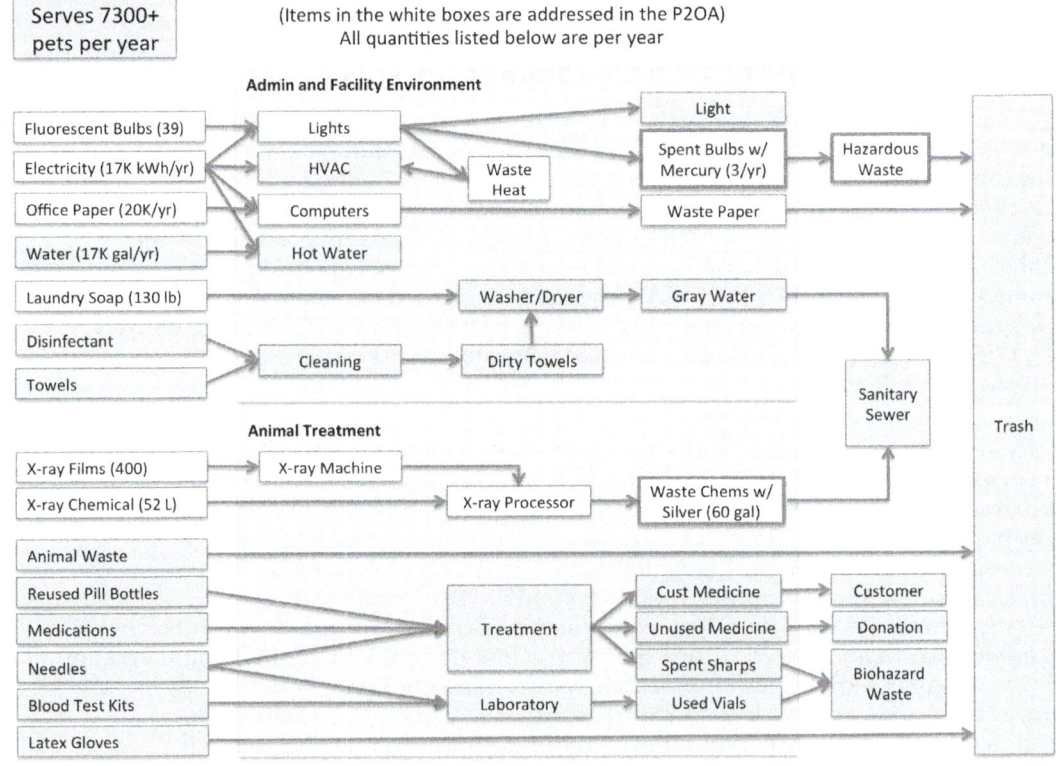

Pollution Prevention Opportunity Assessment
Worksheet 2
Materials Flow Diagram

Date: May 1, 2014 **P2OA ID Code:** P2OA-2014-01 **Facility:** Animal Hospital
Activity: Veterinarian services of domestic animals

Chemical Inputs	
Name	**Qty.**
Aluminum sufate	6 L
Chemblend Fixer	52 L
Alcohol	
Peroxide	
Chlorohexidine	

Material and Water Inputs	
Name	**Qty.**
X-ray film	400
Foam Quat cleaner	52 cans
Water	17,000 gals
Fluorescent bulbs	3 tubes
Laundry soap	130 lbs
Paper	20,000 sheets

Energy Inputs	
Name	**Qty.**
Electricity of which	17,000 kWh
Lighting	3,332 kWh

Activity
Operations of Vet Clinic

Activity Time Period
One Year

Hazardous Chemical Waste Output	
Name	**Qty.**
Waste x-ray chemicals with	60 gals
Silver	252 g
Fluorescents with	3 tubes
Mercury	9-24 mg

Non-Hazardous Solid Waste Output	
Name	**Qty.**
Paper	20,000 sheets

Waste Water Output	
Name	**Qty.**
Greywater from laundry with	
1,4-Dioxane	

Product or Result Output	
Name	**Qty.**
Laboratory tests	300
Blood/urine tests	300
Medical dips	20
Surgery	260
Routine vet care	7,300

Other	
Name	**Qty.**

Other	
Name	**Qty.**

> **Pollution Prevention Opportunity Assessment**
> **Worksheet 3**
> **Pollution Prevention Opportunity Description**
>
> **Date:** May 1, 2014   **P2OA ID Code:** P2OA-2014-01   **Facility:** Animal Hospital
> **Activity:** Veterinarian services of domestic animals
> **P2O No.** 1   **P2O Title:** Retrofitting fluorescent light fixtures with LED lighting

Current Practice

At this time, the Animal Hospital is equipped with 60-watt incandescent light fixtures, 40-watt 2-ft "U" style, and 32-watt 4-ft tube style fluorescent lights and fixtures throughout the clinic. There are 16 fluorescent fixtures; of those fixtures, 14 are large 4-ft fixtures with 2-4 fluorescent tube-lights per fixture and another two small 2-ft "U" style fixtures with two fluorescent tube-lights per fixture. The high traffic rooms are illuminated approximately 10 hrs a day and lower traffic approximately 6 hrs a day. They replace about three fluorescent tube-lights a year that burn out. The current method of disposal for spent tubes is in the trash.

Recommended Action

Retrofitting the fluorescent lights with light emitting diode (LED) lights while utilizing the existing fixtures. Necessary action would be the removal of ballasts (free recycling available locally) and rewiring the sockets of all 16 fluorescent fixtures to accommodate T8, LED lights. LED lighting uses significantly less energy than incandescent and last up to 10 times longer than fluorescent lighting, thus saving money. "Energy Star" designation for linear fluorescent lamps and their solid-state retrofits is not available. Additionally, replacement of the two currently used 60-watt incandescent light bulbs with comparable LED replacement bulbs into existing fixtures is recommended. These two fixtures are located in the dark room/storage and laundry/bathroom. Replacement of incandescent light bulbs with LED comparable bulbs may yield a 90% reduction in energy use.

When selecting LED replacements it is important to look for manufacturers with a recognized name for quality lighting products. When selecting LEDs it is also important to note that they are directional light sources and thus need appropriate fixtures for the light to be distributed well in a space. Also, there are a variety of colors and a desired light color needs to be selected based on the application and personal preference.

A qualified electrician could rewire the existing fixtures for LED lights to be used. Calls to two electricians suggested 30 minutes per fixture would be needed to retrofit. Research online found cost efficient LED bulbs with lumen levels comparable to existing fluorescent tubes.

Solid State Lighting technology is changing rapidly. The information in this assessment represents the information available for this specific application at the time of the assessment. If there is a delay in implementation it would be important for the lighting market to be re-assessed.

NOTE: this opportunity will assess and calculate costs for replacement of all 16 fluorescent fixtures. Though not considered, replacement of only frequently used rooms, reception area, technician area, surgical room, kennel, x-ray room, and the three exam rooms would also yield a cost savings.

Calculation of Waste Reduction and/or Energy Savings

- The vet clinic currently uses approximately 3332 kWh per year for lighting energy.
- A 47 percent energy savings would be possible by installing LED lights.
- The new LED energy would be approximately 1762 kWh per year for LED lighting.
- Current fluorescent lighting contains mercury and can require Hazardous Waste disposal when in large quantities at a cost of approximately $2.00 per year. Free drop off of tubes is available at the County landfill and local electronics store.
- Waste reduction of mercury would be 100% as LED's contain no mercury. Although, not within the scope of this assessment, a typical 4-ft fluorescent light has 3-8mg of mercury, which if not properly recycled will bio-accumulate in the food chain, in the soil and water environment

⇒ **Total energy reduction due to LED light conversion is 1570 kWh per year (more than one month's current total electric usage)**

3332 kWh/yr (current) –1762 kWh/yr (LED energy) = 1570 kWh/yr energy savings

Calculation of Annual Cost Savings

- Current fluorescent energy usage costs for the Animal Hospital lighting is approximately 3332 kWh per year at $0.10 cents per kWh3332 kWh/yr x $0.10 kWh = $333.20/yr (fluorescent energy costs)
- Converting all 16 fluorescent fixtures to LED, new annual energy cost of $176.20 per yearLED lighting 1762 kWh/yr x $0.10 kWh = $176.20/yr (LED energy costs)
- Currently the Animal Hospital replaces about two fluorescent lights per year at a cost of about $8.98

⇒ **Total annual energy cost savings due to LED light conversion is $166 per year**

$333.20/yr (current annual cost) - $176.20/yr (LED annual cost) = $157.00/yr energy savings

$157.00/yr (energy) + $8.98 (replacement fluorescent lights) = $165.98 annual savings

Calculation of Implementation Cost and Payback

The implementation cost of this opportunity would involve the purchasing of 35 LED 18W 4-ft and 4 LED 18W 2-ft "U" type lights to achieve comparable lighting in each fixture at the Animal Hospital. This would require an electrician to disconnect the existing fluorescent ballasts currently in each fixture and rewire the sockets for each fixture for the LED lights to operate. Most LED lights bulbs have built in drivers thus additional drivers are not needed.

- LED, T8-18W 4-ft would cost a total of $840.00 ($24 each) for a supply of 35 LED lights
- LED, T8-18W 2-ft would cost a total of $147.80 ($36.95 each) for a supply of 4 LED lights
- Labor to remove fluorescent ballasts and install LED T8 lights in 16 fixtures is approximately $350
- Donation of functioning fluorescent tubes to a charity like the local food pantry, Sharing & Caring, Inc. would achieve minimal waste for this opportunity.

⇒ **The implementation cost of this opportunity by purchasing new "Clear Cover" lenses, LED tube style, T8, lights would be to $1338**

$840.00 (4-ft lights) + $147.80 (2-ft lights) + $350.00 (labor) = $1337.80

NOTE: In some fixtures, it may be possible to install only one LED light in the fixture but this issue was not explored. If desired, recommendation is to use a higher wattage LED, such as a T8-23W 4-ft light (cost $36.99 each), the increased wattage will illuminate better. This LED is equivalent to a 65W fluorescent.

The payback is 8 years.

⇒ **$1338 (implementation cost) / $166/year (annual savings) = 8 years**

NOTE: Due to the length of payback time for this opportunity, a supplemental opportunity, that would decrease the payback time, would be to convert some or individual light fixtures as they become inoperable. Due to the age of the building and/or light fixtures at the vet clinic it is inevitable that the existing fluorescent ballasts will stop operating. When this happens, the LED conversion would be incremental and have a shorter payback time. Thus by reducing the number of replacement bulbs required at one time, it would drop the implementation cost and increase the energy savings; e.g. fewer LED bulbs = less electricity used. This supplemental opportunity might incur a higher implementation cost due to additional electrician service calls but is a favorable implementation consideration. *If LED retrofit is done incrementally, the fixtures containing LED lights must be labeled "LED ONLY" to avoid confusion with fluorescent bulbs.*

Additionally, as LED technology improves, the cost of each LED light will continue to go down (not factoring in that energy cost will increase over time). The cost of LED lights has already reduced over 50% in less than two years. Thus if a per unit cost for each LED light was around $10, the payback period would be under 5 years based on today's dollars.

> **Pollution Prevention Opportunity Assessment**
> **Worksheet 3**
> **Pollution Prevention Opportunity Description**
>
> **Date:** May 1, 2014 **P2OA ID Code:** P2OA-2014-01 **Facility:** Animal Hospital
> **Activity:** Veterinarian services of domestic animals
> **P2O No.** 2 **P2O Title:** Purchase of a digital x-ray machine

Current Practice

At this time, the Animal Hospital processes x-rays for domestic animals on a Konica Medical Processor (model SRX-101A) film machine. The clinic processes about 400 images a year using this equipment. The machine requires supplies and a monthly service call for calibration and cleaning. Additionally, the film processing requires developer and fixer chemicals that once a month are disposed of as wastewater. Residual silver remaining in the developer/fixer solution, resulting from the film processing is not recovered from these chemicals during disposal.

Recommended Action

The recommended action is to replace the film x-ray machine with a digital x-ray machine. This action would decrease energy costs, waste disposal, labor costs, toxic silver disposal, and subsequent environmental impacts resulting from the current film processing wastewater discharge. Additional benefits include better patient care as digital images go directly to a patient's file and reduced x-ray exposure resulting from occasional retakes of ineffective x-rays. Digital images can be highly manipulated for contrast, exposure, and enlargements. An unintended benefit is the removal of the dark room currently used for film processing and storage space needed for film x-ray processing. Finally, service calls would reduce from monthly to approximately every 2 years.

Calculation of Waste Reduction and/or Energy Savings

- The vet clinic currently uses approximately 3432 kWh per year of electricity for the x-ray machine; it is running for approximately 10 hours per day for 260 days per year.
- The new digital x-ray machine would use approximately 7.92 kWh per year to operate it.
- A 99.8 percent energy savings would be achieved by installing a digital x-ray machine.
- Currently approximately 60 gal per year of waste solution from the x-ray film developer/fixer is disposed of to the sewer without recovery of trace silver.
- Source reduction of silver from wastewater would be 100%, realized immediately with digital x-ray machine implementation.

⇒ **Total annual energy savings from digital x-ray machine use is 3424 kWh per year.**

3432kWh/yr (current) − 7.92 kWh/yr (digital energy) = 3424.08 kWh/yr (energy saved)

Calculation of Annual Cost Savings

- Current energy usage costs for the vet clinic's film x-ray machine is approximately 3432 kWh per year at $0.10 cents per kWh.12Amps x 110V = 1320W / 1000k = 1.32kW X 10hr/day x 260 days/yr = 3432kWh/yr3432 kWh/yr x $0.10 kWh = $343.26/yr (film x-ray energy costs)

- By converting to digital x-rays, the new annual energy cost of $0.79 per yr.4Amps x 110V = 440W / 1000k = .44kW x 18hr/yr = 7.92 kWh/yr7.92 kWh/yr (digital energy) x $0.10 kWh = $0.79/yr (digital energy costs)

- The Animal Hospital's approximate yearly purchase of x-ray supplies; 10x12 film, 14x17 film, x-ray jackets, lights for the machine, developer/fixer Bi-packs are a total of $600.
- Service charges by Bay X-ray, Inc. are $75 per month, totaling $900 per year.
- It is estimated that it takes the Animal Hospital staff 5 minutes to process a film x-ray currently, resulting in a $400 yearly labor cost associated with the use of dark room x-ray film processing.
- Currently approximately 400 x-ray images are done a year. Assuming 10% of x-rays currently done are retakes thus, 360 images would be the approximately annual digital x-rays performed.

⇒ **Total annual cost savings due to digital x-ray implementation is $2242 per year.**

$343.26/yr (current energy) – $0.79/yr (digital energy) = $342.47/yr energy savings

$342.47/yr energy savings + $600 (supplies) + $900 (service) + $400 (labor) = $2242.47

Calculation of Implementation Cost and Payback

- The implementation cost of this opportunity would involve purchase of a "CARESTREAM Vita CR Systems" (digital x-ray machine brand suggested by current Tech) for $17,250.
- Installation and training for this machine may have a one-time cost of $250.

⇒ **The implementation cost of purchasing a digital x-ray machine would be to $17,500.**

$17,250 + $250 (installation & training labor) = $17,500

The payback is 7 years and 10 months.

⇒ **$17,500 (implementation cost) / $2242/year (annual cost savings) = 7 years & 10 months**

Pollution Prevention Opportunity Assessment
Worksheet 3
Pollution Prevention Opportunity Description

Date: May 1, 2014 **P2OA ID Code:** P2OA-2014-01 **Facility:** Animal Hospital
Activity: Veterinarian services of domestic animals
P2O No. 3 **P2O Title:** Purchasing of concentrated, biodegradable laundry detergent

Current Practice

At this time, the staff of the Animal Hospital wash soiled items, such as towels and blankets that are used daily for routine care, surgery, and cleaning of the facility. They have an onsite washer and dryer available for this use. Currently they use a standard commercial powder for laundry detergent, which recommends 2.6 oz. of detergent per load.

Recommended Action

To replace currently used laundry detergent with concentrated, biodegradable laundry detergent that contains no 1,4-Dioxane, formaldehyde or photochemical content. One such example is locally available detergent with coconut-based fabric softener. Plant-based, environmentally friendly products are readily available to consumers and reduce harmful pollutants from entering the waste stream thus reducing the impact on wastewater treatment facilities.

Additionally the use of concentrated detergents results in more detergent loads per bottle of detergent, reducing the need to purchase additional bottles, thus reducing the manufacturing of additional bottles and subsequent transportation costs of those bottles compared to non-concentrated detergents.

Calculation of Waste Reduction and/or Energy Savings

- The vet clinic currently uses commercial powder detergent that recommends 2.6 oz. of detergent per load of wash. This leads to the purchase of 4 buckets per year.
- It is recommended that if the Animal Hospital used a concentrated, environmentally friendly laundry detergent this would lead to a waste reduction of current detergent by 1 bucket (14.7 kg) per year the manufacturer's recommended rate of 0.8 oz per load.

⇒ **Total annual waste reduction due to the use of concentrated, environmentally friendly laundry detergent is 14.7 kg (32.5 lbs) or 1 less bucket to purchase per year.**

Calculation of Annual Cost Savings

- The vet clinic currently pays approximately $14.88 per bottle of non-concentrated laundry detergent capable of providing 200 wash loads for a top loading machine.

- They wash approximately 15 loads per week x 52 weeks for 780 loads per year; thus the number of non-concentrated laundry detergent buckets purchased per year is approximately 4.780 loads/yr / 200 loads per bucket = 3.9 buckets = 4$14.88/bucket X 4 buckets/yr = $59.52/yr (current detergent costs)

- The cost of an environmentally friendly laundry detergent is $13.98 per bottle of concentrated laundry detergent capable of providing 252 wash loads
- By changing to a concentrated, environmentally friendly laundry detergent they would need to purchase 3 bottles resulting in a new annual cost of $41.94/yr

⇒ **Total annual cost savings due to concentrated, environmentally friendly, laundry detergent implementation is $18 per year.**

$59.52/yr (current detergent costs) - $41.94/yr (eco detergent costs) = $17.58/yr savings

Calculation of Implementation Cost and Payback

- With this opportunity, there would be no additional implementation costs, as it is a simple substitution to a concentrated, environmentally friendly laundry detergent. This opportunity could be implemented at any time.
- The new detergent can be purchased at the same store where they buy their existing detergent.

⇒ **The payback is immediate.**

Since there is no implementation cost with this opportunity, payback is immediate.

> **Pollution Prevention Opportunity Assessment**
> **Worksheet 3**
> **Pollution Prevention Opportunity Description**
>
> **Date:** May 1, 2014 **P2OA ID Code:** P2OA-2014-01 **Facility:** Animal Hospital
> **Activity:** Veterinarian services of domestic animals
> **P2O No.** 4 **P2O Title:** Purchasing of recycled paper products and use of duplexing

Current Practice

At this time, the front staff of the Animal Hospital uses copier paper daily for printing of patient receipts and records. They have an onsite printer available for this use. Currently they use approximately 20,000 sheets (40 reams) of copier paper per year. This copier paper has 0% of recyclable content. Copier paper is purchased as needed, by the case (10 reams/case).

Recommended Action

It is recommended for the Animal Hospital to use up current supply of copier paper and then begin buying copier paper containing 100% recycled content. Copier paper made from recycled post-consumer waste (labeled on packaging as 100% PCW) is equal in brightness and functionality for multiple uses. Use of 100% PCW reduces pollution, natural resources and has economic benefits.

Additional, immediate cost savings can be achieved by utilizing the duplexing feature on printers and printing double-sided documents in place of single sided whenever possible. It is estimated that 15% of printed documents and receipts require more than one sheet of paper. The use of duplexing would reduce the amount of paper needing to be purchased.

Calculation of Waste Reduction and/or Energy Savings

- Currently the Animal Hospital purchases approximately 20,000 sheets of paper per year.
- An estimated 15% of printed documents and receipts could be duplexed per year resulting in a waste reduction of 3,000 sheets of paper per year.

⇒ **Total annual waste reduction due to duplexed document implementation is 3,000 sheets or 6 reams per year.**

Calculation of Annual Cost Savings

- Currently the vet clinic purchases approximately 40 reams of paper per year at an average cost of $3.19 per ream for a current annual cost of $127.60 per year.$3.19 (cost/ream) x 40 reams of paper = $127.60 (current paper cost)

- The purchase of 100% recycled copier paper (100% PCW) for $5.99 per ream (cost/ream) for a recycled paper annual cost of $203.87 per year.$5.99 (cost/ream) x 40 reams of paper = $203.87 (recycled paper cost)

- The cost of waste reduction from 3000 sheets of paper (6 reams), due to duplexing multi page documents and receipts is $19.14 per year.$3.19 (cost/ream) x 6 reams of paper = $19.14 (cost savings from duplexing)

⇒ **Total annual cost increase by implementation of using 100% recycled paper and duplexing is $57 per year.**

$127.60 (current paper 0% PCW) - $203.87 (100% PCW paper cost) = - ($76.27) - $76.27 + $19.14 (duplexing savings) = - ($57.13) increased costs for recycled paper

Calculation of Implementation Cost and Payback

⇒   **There is no implementation cost for changing the purchasing policy to recycled paper**

⇒ **There is no implementation cost for duplexing, as it is just a change in procedure.**

Note: No appreciable price difference ($0.31 per ream) between 50% PCW and 100% PCW

⇒ **There is no payback.**

Since the annual costs with this opportunity are higher than the current costs, there is no payback.

Pollution Prevention Opportunity Assessment
Worksheet 4
Pollution Prevention Opportunities Summary

Date: May 1, 2014 **P2OA ID Code:** P2OA-2014-01 **Facility:** Animal Hospital
Activity: Veterinarian services of domestic animals

P2O No.	P2O Title	Waste Class Reduced	Annual Waste Reduction or Energy Savings	Estimated Annual Cost Savings	Estimated Implementation Cost	Payback
1	Retrofitting florescent light fixtures with LED bulbs	Hazardous Waste	1,570 kWh	$166	$1,338	8 years
2	Purchasing a digital x-ray machine	Process sewer	60 gals 3,424 kWh	$2,242	$17,500	7 years & 10 months
3	Purchasing of biodegradable laundry soap	Process sewer	14.7 kg	$18	None	Immediate
4	Purchasing of recycled paper products and use of duplexing	Sanitary	3,000 sheets	$(57)	None	None

Other Brainstorming Opportunities Considered but Not Analyzed

The following energy reducing ideas are considered best practices but would bring minimal cost savings so were not analyzed:

- Use of power strips for all office equipment will prevent electricity usage after hours. Computers and battery chargers draw power even when they are turned off unless you unplug them or use a power strip. Use low power/sleep modes on computers to save energy and keep them cooler which reduces A/C usage.
- Purchase of Energy Star-labeled computer/office equipment can use 30-65% less energy than computers without this designation.
- Installing motion light sensors in infrequently used rooms like office and supply/storage area.

The following environmentally friendly procurement opportunities are also considered best practices but would bring minimal cost savings so were not analyzed:

- Purchase paper towels with post-consumer waste (PCW) recycled content.
- Switch to environmentally/earth friendly cleaning products.

The following opportunity would viable but purchasing a digital x-ray machine is a preferable approach since it is source reduction instead of recycling:

- Recycle old x-ray films and chemical waste solution from developing process with a silver recycler.

> ## Pollution Prevention Opportunity Assessment
> ## Worksheet 5
> ## Final Summary
>
> **Date:** May 1, 2014 **P2OA ID Code:** P2OA-2014-01 **Facility:** Animal Hospital
> **Activity:** Veterinarian services of domestic animals

Proposed Opportunities and Discussion

In opportunity #1, the replacement of fluorescent lighting will have a 47% reduction in energy cost resulting in an estimated annual savings of $166 when compared to currently used lighting. This opportunity will have a reduction of 1570 kWh, which is more than the average annual monthly electric bill usage. The implementation costs of $1338 has a payback period of 8 years but that calculation does not include any further reductions from building improvement tax credits and possible tax deductions under the Energy Independence Act of 2007.

In opportunity #2, the purchase of a digital x-ray machine would not only yield an annual cost savings of $2,242, but also the substantial energy reduction of 3424 kWh per year. Other benefits are the elimination of film developing labor costs, ability to do automated record keeping, and reduced worker exposure to x-rays and chemicals. The environmental benefit by eliminating the chemical waste disposal that contains highly toxic silver is an important unrealized benefit to this opportunity. This opportunity has an implementation cost of $17,500 with a payback of 7 years and 10 months while not assessing other tax benefits that might be realized by a business.

In opportunity #3, a product substitution for currently used laundry detergent to a plant-based concentrated laundry detergent with no 1,4-Dioxane, formaldehyde or photochemical content, will yield an annual cost savings of $18. Use of compounds containing 1,4-Dioxane (a known carcinogen) results in additional treatment costs of the polluted wastewater. The annual waste reduction of a 14.7 kg bucket will be realized with the use of a concentrated plant-based environmentally friendly detergent. There is no implementation cost associated with this opportunity and payback is immediate.

Finally, opportunity #4 is the substitution of currently used copier paper made with 0% post-consumer waste (PCW) to one that is 100% PCW. The Animal Hospital uses approximately 20,000 sheets of paper per year and currently do not duplex any printing. The use of duplexing results in an estimated waste reduction of 3,000 sheets of paper per year, realized just by activating this feature on the printer. Recycled content paper is available online and can be shipped free to the store. The convenience of ordering online is an unrealized cost savings. The cost of recycled paper is slightly higher than the currently used paper thus; this opportunity will have a cost increase of $57 annually.

Recommendations and Schedule for Implementation

It is recommended to implement all four of these opportunities as they offer appreciable cost savings and desirable pollution prevention opportunities. Opportunity #3 is the easiest to implement with no implementation costs and should be done as soon as current supplies of laundry detergent are used. Plant-based laundry detergent and cleaners are highly efficient and beneficial for the environment. This opportunity requires no vendor coordination as it is locally available the store where the Animal Hospital already shops.

Opportunities #1 and #2 should be implemented as soon as possible, especially since they may have possible tax credits and tax deductions available this year. Although they carry longer payback periods, those calculations do not include the possibility of any tax benefits, which would reduce the payback timeframe. They also have the greatest pollution prevention reduction and highest energy cost and energy use reductions. Opportunity #1 (LED lighting) will require coordination with an electrician and ordering the LED lights.

For opportunity #2, the negotiated price of the digital x-ray machine system is highly competitive and is $7750 lower than the quote from the clinics' current vendor. The current vendor may meet this price and the Animal Hospital should negotiate with them about a comparable price for purchase and training, which will help the local economy.

Implementation of opportunity #4 does not include an annual cost savings for the Animal Hospital but current copier paper supplies are low thus it is a good time to implement this opportunity and taking a step towards pollution prevention and reducing the environmental impact on the earth. Additionally, as use of 100% PCW copier paper becomes more accessible the costs will continue to go down resulting in additional cost savings not realized at this time.

ABOUT THE AUTHORS

Jill A. Engel-Cox, Ph.D.

Over her 25-year career, Dr. Jill Engel-Cox has been an engineer, researcher, program manager, and strategic planner of a diverse suite of clean technology, renewable energy, and environmental management programs in the U.S., Asia, and Middle East. Her first job was climbing smokestacks in Los Angeles, followed by leading pollution prevention assessments and programs for small and medium sized businesses and R&D laboratories in Colorado, Washington, Maryland, the District of Columbia, and internationally. Throughout her career, she has sought out opportunities to facilitate science-based environmental outreach and to develop and teach university courses and interactive multi-day workshops, including a graduate level industrial pollution prevention class at two universities. She is author of over 40 peer-reviewed journal and conference publications on technical and policy topics and has co-published two books, one on pollution prevention and one on stakeholder communications. Her full profile can be found on LinkedIn.

Kim M. Fowler

Ms. Kim Fowler is a senior research engineer at the Pacific Northwest National Laboratory in Richland, Washington. Her research has included assessing the environmental, social, and economic impacts of process, product, and facility designs and operations; establishing new environmental programs; identifying opportunities for federal agency greenhouse gas management; and evaluating processes for efficiency. Her most recent work is focused on whole building performance measurement where she developed a method for Federal and commercial buildings and has measured over 75 different buildings for energy use, water use, operations and maintenance, waste and recycling, occupant commute, and occupant satisfaction with the building attributes. She has taught multiple courses at Washington State University in the Environmental Science Department and has been a U.S. Green Building Council Leadership in Energy and Environmental Design (LEED) accredited professional since 2003. She has co-authored 2 books, 4 book chapters, and many journal articles and technical reports. Her full profile can be found on LinkedIn.

Other Publications by the Same Authors

A Communications Guide for Sustainable Development: How Interested Parties Become Partners, 2ⁿᵈ Edition, Gretchen Hund, Jill Engel-Cox, and Kim Fowler

A Communications Guide for Sustainable Development
How Interested Parties Become Partners

2nd Edition

Society
Industry
Environment
Partners

Gretchen Hund, Jill Engel-Cox, and Kim Fowler

Made in the USA
Monee, IL
14 July 2023